UNMASKED
Real People from
Montgomery County, Texas

Copyright © 2011 Good Catch Publishing, Beaverton, OR.

All rights reserved. Written permission must be secured from the publisher to use or reproduce any part of this book, except for brief quotations in critical reviews or articles.

This book was written for the express purpose of conveying the love and mercy of Jesus Christ. The statements in this book are substantially true; however, names and minor details have been changed to protect people and situations from accusation or incrimination.

All Scripture quotations, unless otherwise noted, are taken from the New International Version Copyright 1973, 1987, 1984 by International Bible Society.

Published in Beaverton, Oregon, by Good Catch Publishing.
www.goodcatchpublishing.com
V1.1

Printed in the United States of America

Table of Contents

	Dedication	9
	Acknowledgements	11
	Introduction	15
1	The Roughest Ward	17
2	The Hornet's Nest	45
3	Small Town Tales	75
4	Closing the Book	103
5	Core Value	119
6	Attacked	139
7	Rebel Rider	155
	Conclusion	193

DEDICATION

Unmasked
is dedicated to all of those people who,
for various reasons, have felt that they have
to hold up an image or strength or a certain status.
This book is dedicated to YOU.

ACKNOWLEDGEMENTS

I would like to thank Kenny Martin, Sr., for his vision for this book and for his hard work in making it a reality. And to the people of Upper Room, thank you for your boldness and vulnerability in sharing your personal stories.

This book would not have been published without the amazing efforts of our Project Manager and editor, Marla Lindstrom Benroth. Her untiring resolve pushed this project forward and turned it into a stunning victory. Thank you for your great fortitude and diligence. Deep thanks to our incredible Editor in Chief, Michelle Cuthrell, and Executive Editor, Nicole Phinney Lowell, for all the amazing work they do. I would also like to thank our invaluable proofreader, Melody Davis, for the focus and energy she has put into perfecting our words.

Lastly, I want to extend our gratitude to the creative and very talented Ann Clayton, who designed the beautiful cover for *UNMASKED: Real People from Montgomery County, Texas.*

Daren Lindley
President and CEO
Good Catch Publishing

The book you are about to read
is a compilation of authentic life stories.
The facts are true, and the events are real.
These storytellers have dealt with crisis, tragedy, abuse
and neglect and have shared their most private moments,
mess-ups and hang-ups in order for others to learn and
grow from them. In order to protect the identities of those
involved in their pasts, the names and details of some
storytellers have been withheld or changed.

INTRODUCTION

We live in a society that revolves around entertainment: what movie is coming out next, who is playing in it and what role do they play. Where we hear lines like "get over it" or "take one for the team," "suck it up and let's keep rolling" over and over again.

This causes us to be people that we really aren't. Peer pressure causes our teens and even our children to uphold images, and in doing so, we wear masks. We have a mask for our boss (teacher), mask for our spouse (girlfriend/boyfriend/parents), mask for our friends and a mask for the public. The problem comes when we wear masks so long that nobody really knows who we are, and we don't know if there is anything at all that can make us not feel this way anymore.

The stories in this book are true stories of real people who have made mistakes, experienced difficult challenges or were victims of insensitive things that have brought them some of life's greatest difficulties. Their stories are raw, humbling and heart wrenching, yet true.

The people whom these things happened to are not perfect. You will not read of them riding off into the sunset on the white horse with the prince or beauty queen. These are people who wore masks, and they learned to take them off and live a life of hope and joy without them.

THE ROUGHEST WARD
The Story of Kenny and Virginia Martin
Written by Richard Drebert

Kenny:

If he got to my .45, he would kill me.

We writhed on the barroom floor, slick with beer and blood. I gouged, kicked and kneed — but the man was stronger. I felt his legs lock around my waist as he smashed me over and over with one boney fist. His other hand groped down my right hip to my leather holster, and we shared a moment of truth.

I jammed my hand into a painful place, squeezing with all my might, praying for agony to channel past the booze to his brain, and suddenly he shoved away, howling, like he was repulsed by my badge. I cuffed one brawny wrist on the fly and barely secured the other before I heard the shell chambered.

Did the suspect have a friend?

My holster was already unsnapped; I drew my Colt and pulled his face close to mine. I shoved my pistol's cool barrel against his ear, *hard.*

"If I *see* that shotgun, you're a dead man. Got it?"

We stumbled out of the bar, and comrades in blue deposited the man in a cruiser while I assessed my bruises — I'd be hurtin' tomorrow.

UNMASKED

"I heard someone rack a shotgun, but I couldn't see it. Pretty dark in there ..."

Officers now crossed the bar's threshold to jar loose versions of the "truth." I had answered a call from the bar manager about someone who stiffed the bartender and then fell asleep on a stool. When I woke the man, he leaped on me like a grizzly, and the fight was on.

Now I sat in a patrol car, a little dazed, thinking how lucky I was that he didn't pull a knife. I had just successfully blown past my year's probation as a police officer working the notorious 5th Ward in Houston, Texas, a nationally reputed breeding ground for vice and victims.

From the bar, officers were marching out a wizened elderly black woman, and a cop behind her wore a grin as he proudly carried her scuffed-up sawed-off shotgun. The old woman grinned, too, right at me.

"Baby, y'all think I wuz gonna shoot *YOUR* a**?"

"Yes, ma'am, I did."

My cohorts in blue were studying us like we starred in a great beer commercial.

"Nawww!" she said, throwing her arms in the air. "I got out that shotgun 'cause I wuz gonna teach that son of a b**** ya *don't* jump *no* police!"

It was a tableau for all of us to remember — one of the few times a citizen stood up for a police officer in the hostile 5th Ward. More often than not, the *victims* even hated to see a badge.

At 20 years old, I was rewarded with a loyalty from

THE ROUGHEST WARD

these men, veteran officers, often murdered by the ones they were sworn to protect. They called me brother.

Soon I agreed with their judgment of the world around us: It was all going to hell in a hand basket. And this included my marriage. I embraced their unwritten code without question: *If you're not wearing blue, you must be sh***.

Virginia:

In my early 20s, I was in a party mood — damaged goods from Humble, Texas.

Each morning I drove 40 miles to Houston for work at the constable's office, where I was "Jill-of-all-trades" — the girl at the counter who knew where everything was filed. My self-esteem lived at the Harris County Courthouse in those days, but when I was alone, I felt used, polluted — Seth had seen to that.

I was barely 18, never dreaming that a local boy would "drug" me to numb my moral defenses and rape me.

I had scraped up my courage and confronted Seth.

"What? Come on, I never did nothin' to you!"

Was I wrong? Had I dreamed it? It took months, but I finally pieced together the truth like a shattered mirror, and I gazed at my misshapen image *every* day since. Who would have believed a silly Sunday school girl, anyway? Maybe Mother, who struggled with three jobs and four children … but what could she have done? I confided in a girlfriend, and I knew I had to try to just "get past it." At least I had *memories* of being a good girl …

UNMASKED

Party mood. Dancing and drinking with friends helped me reassert my "woman's *right* to choose" and say NO to a man! Or "yes," if I felt like it — and "yes" got me pregnant.

God was really pissed off, now. All the years he had invested in me — from the nursery to Bible camps — shaped by perfect church attendance so that little Baptist girls of Humble could follow in my footsteps ...

All bets were off now.

"Hon, it's not *life* until there's a heartbeat."

I sat in the Planned Parenthood office, my own heart slamming my chest, searching for a way out of consequences. The "embryo's" daddy wanted nothing to do with me anymore. What if I lost my job? And what would people think of me?

"Don't sentence yourself to the misery of raising an unwanted child. It won't be fair to either of you ..."

The lady was *so* nice and helped me make an appointment for my abortion. The ache in my soul came the evening my baby was taken.

Party on.

Kenny:

I stood on the porch, humiliated.

"Eleven years old, and still wetting the bed?! Young man, shame! You just stay out here." The screen door slammed, and I slumped into a patio chair. Boys and girls in the cul-de-sac stared, covered their mouths and laughed as I tried to hide.

THE ROUGHEST WARD

A diaper. Me! This is my punishment for having an accident? My stomach felt like I swallowed a barbell as anger welled inside me. *Mom* did this. I could just ... kill her!

"Hey, Diaper Boy!"

I forgot Mom. My eyes dropped to my thighs, and I winced. How could I ever face my friends again? Rage churned inside me again — the same rage I would feel as a police officer, when I arrested a pimp or child molester. The same rage I would harbor after I discovered my wife with another man; I was a hair's breadth from finding myself on the wrong side of prison bars.

☙☙☙

In my senior year at Roscommon High School, law enforcement entered my bloodstream when I rode along with Jack Biggar, the chief of the township police department. It was customary for kids plotting an uphill climb to the police academy to answer dispatches with officers as work experience. The big man in a blue uniform mentored me, a boy starved for a man's affirmation.

Dad had been over-occupied much of my growing-up years with hours of overtime as a machine mechanic at plants like Chrysler and Ford Motor. Mom stayed home, lonely, managing my brother and me. She worked at the Baptist church as a volunteer, and sometimes Dad was an usher, when he wasn't away at ball games.

UNMASKED

Dad loved his church softball tourneys, and I stepped right into his baseball cleats as a school jock. And slipped on a football jersey. Then hiked up basketball shorts for a time, until Dad's belittling as our coach ripped off any joy. He had been an all-American, and I never measured up, but we won it all that year.

Mom divorced Dad. She remarried, and Dad seemed to soften some, pining over what he had lost. I spent time with him during this troubled season of life, and he finally remarried. I wasn't motivated by any deep sense of kindness from the Man Upstairs in those days. In fact, I had scrapped religion on the school playground in eighth grade, right after our family imploded. No one at the church we went to even knew Mom and Dad were having trouble — or no one cared.

"I don't get it, God. Why let my mom do this? She works in the church nursery. Dad's an usher. My grandpa is the church treasurer. Is it my fault? Do you think I'm too fat? What's the matter with my family? What's the matter with *me*?"

So many questions — and not one soul in my church of 1,400 took the time to read the questions screaming in a broken little boy's eyes. It was too risky: I was diseased by DIVORCE.

"Go get Sammy. I don't want him sitting with Kenny anymore." My best friend's mother whispered it to her husband, and I heard. It sank deeply into my psyche, and a twisted resolve set as hard as stone: "If *this* is what God is like, I don't need him."

THE ROUGHEST WARD

Besides, I had friends now who liked me. And they offered sweeter enticements by far: weed, sex, liquor — approval.

I stayed away from church, except an occasional foray with my grandmother, a woman who was kind and loving and who I desperately wanted to please. But long after I graduated from high school, I refused to let the religious hypocrites under my skin — for me, *they* had a disease now.

❧❧❧

"Son, when a police officer does something wrong, we stick him on a polygraph. He tells me the truth or gives me a d*** good reason why he failed it. Son, you failed."

It seemed like a deal breaker before I even started. How could I get into the Houston Police Academy if I failed the lie detector? I had already applied at the Troy, Michigan, police department, and my application had died. I had applied at Southfield, Michigan, and it died. I had applied at Ferndale, and that one died.

But Houston had called me in! I flew in an airplane for the first time, on my own dime, and walked from my motel to the Houston Police Department where I found Sergeant Fox.

Under the sergeant's steely gaze, I rifled my mind for an errant falsehood, but came up shiny-clean.

"Sergeant Fox, I don't know why I failed. I told the truth."

UNMASKED

"The machine says you lied when we asked if you stole something."

I paused, reaching deep for control. "I'm manager of a theater back home, with five showings a night. I deposit $10,000 to $15,000 a night sometimes. And I've never been a penny short. You can verify it."

My face was hot, and it wasn't the Texas sun. I shifted uncomfortably in a pool of sweaty silence as Sergeant Fox took my measure.

"Okay," was all he said.

I left the room, deflated, and flew back to Detroit, where I worked — and Houston detectives were suddenly all over me. Questioning former and present employers, school teachers, friends, family.

"Can you start training in eight weeks?" Sergeant Fox's voice seemed almost friendly over the phone. "You passed your background checks."

I closed out accounts, kissed my girlfriend, Christa, goodbye and flew off to Houston with $550 in my wallet and a suitcase. I was 19.

༺༺༺

"You're old enough to save the world, but too young to buy bullets …" In my 16 weeks of make-or-break drills and training, former Army Ranger Peacock was inspirational and stone-hard on his cadets. "There's a big difference between *pain* and *hurt*. Pain is when you're in the back of an ambulance bleeding, heading for the

THE ROUGHEST WARD

hospital. Hurt is JUST IN YOUR MIND! Suck it up!"

I graduated top of my class, and they gave me a choice of Houston police stations. For me, it was no contest. One station stood out like the goal after a 30-yard catch.

"If you don't fit in at the Northeast Station, they'll shoot you in the back."

This was where the action was.

So the rookie rode the 5th Ward, patrolling the bowels of Houston each evening, and living the fool with an unfaithful wife, whom I could never love enough to satisfy.

Virginia:

You'd think I might have learned.

But a woman whose life is wrapped up in herself can be self-destructive in her search for a meaningful life. This time I didn't seek counsel from someone whose salary was tied to the blood of frightened girls and babies. I let my beautiful daughter be *born*, pink and lovely. Jenn's innocence changed my direction — innocence I experienced again and again through her. I determined that my girl would NEVER know the pain I had. It suited me fine that her father wasn't interested in Jenn.

I had a great job, good benefits and help from my mom, as she could, whom I had supported when she was in need. After a difficult divorce while I was a sophomore, Mom had needed me to care for my brothers and sisters while she worked. Now she stepped in to help me. I went back to Humble, Texas, with my baby girl.

UNMASKED

I found that my faith had roots after all. My hard knocks had only dusted off the abiding hopes I had for Jenn and myself. Now, if I could somehow convince God that I was worth another try ...

Kenny:

I stalked the streets on nightshift patrol in the most notorious, crime-ridden district in the nation, except, maybe, the Bronx: the 5th Ward. *Perfect.* If there was a God, he had abandoned Houston's district to the devil and his gangs north of Buffalo Bayou.

My first call as a rookie-in-training was a double shooting, at a house where two "brothers" were drinking hard and long. One man sat with his hands around a mass hanging from his belly; the other curled next to him, fiddling with two leaky red holes in his abdomen.

This was no ride-along.

"Call it in," my partner groused, and I heard my own *officer's* voice report the macabre scene, requesting an ambulance.

"They aren't long for this world." He pointed at one: "Shotgun." He nodded at the other: ".357 slugs."

Houston's inner city at night has a seductive, desensitizing effect on police officers, drinking in the ambience of death while on patrol.

A rookie officer in the 5th finally hardens to the mayhem or must bulk up an immunity with some "force" to shield him from the corruption that rails against his soul. For pimps and whores, drug dealers and gangs, life is

THE ROUGHEST WARD

penny-cheap (at least when it's not their own), and a palpable lust clings to every drop of Texas sweat — even if you wear blue.

When my wife, Christa, hit the streets as a rookie police officer, she ran wild. She had joined me in Houston before I finished the academy, and in months she vamped a new spin upon "to have and to hold" — among my fellow officers. She graduated the police academy, too, but the seductive Houston streets lured her away.

For years I had shut down any hope for God's mercy in my life. I had interred the need for Jesus in junior high when his church scorned my family, but in my fury at Christa and her lovers, I felt dread penetrate my God-proof vest. I prayed desperately for a change in her heart, knowing that deadly distractions patrolled my mind. My partner depended upon me — but I was losing control.

Where is she today, and who is she with? I seethed at my impotence in reining in the chaos in my marriage; divorce documents had been served, but Christa still bedeviled my heart.

"Officer Martin, your wife has been Life Flighted from a rollover accident on Highway …"

My heart sank, then leaped at the thought of a reason to reconcile. I rushed to Christa's bedside, my anger muted by love and concern — her male companion was dead; there were questions about who was driving, and alcohol may have been involved.

In the months that followed, I renewed the vows in my heart for Christa and set aside my body armor so God could touch me again — it was the first time in almost a decade.

My dilemma: As Christa recovered, she still nursed an unspoken contempt for me, much like I felt from the streetwalkers I arrested. We still lived separately, and her interest in religion seemed as closed as her heart when I suggested we seek spiritual help at a church.

"Church is for people who can't handle reality, Kenny."

When my supervising sergeant pulled me aside one day after my shift, my world fell in on itself. Few, if any, affairs are safe from the radar guns of trained police officers.

"Kenny, your wife's messing around on you, again."

I had a hard time digesting his words, and I got defensive. "Christa's still laid up. She doesn't even have a car."

He didn't meet my gaze, like he had just arrested my relative in a sex sting. "Just thought you should know."

Now I had to be sure.

Dressed in black, armed with a sawed-off shotgun with a folding stock and a .45 pistol, I staked out our house as though the woman I loved was a trafficker in cocaine. Hours passed, and I felt relieved — then she came out of the garage on a bicycle. Seething, I followed her to a fellow officer's home and snuck around back to a deck with a hot tub.

I watched them together in revulsion and anguish.

A hair-trigger away from killing them both.

THE ROUGHEST WARD

It would be a crime of passion, and I added up the years I would spend in prison. I was 22 …

Go HOME! The d*** voice in my head crescendoed, and I pried myself from my mission. I turned on my heel and faded into the darkness, images of my wife and the man seared into my mind.

"Remember. Everyone *lies* here in the 5th Ward." It was one of the first lessons I learned as a rookie. No one told the truth when it came to his or her guilt — no one. No one wanted to face the judge. I didn't even try to confront Christa again.

☙☙☙

The bright blood-red Target store was crowded with women when I bought the plastic shower curtain and comforters. I could have been filling a shopping list for my "sweetie," but in reality, I had a date with my Colt.

My back throbbed low and hard as I drove home. Days before I had chased down a car-theft suspect, who hopped a 10-foot fence. In pursuit, at the top of the fence, I lost my balance and plummeted atop a pile of bricks. I ran down the suspect and cuffed him before giving in to the agony. Now, on disability leave, I had time to drink and *think.*

I called Christa one night, and after a short cussing out, she hung up on me — but the phone *didn't* disconnect. Her diatribe continued, and I heard the chuckle from a man in the room. She ended with: "The biggest mistake I ever made was marrying Kenny ..."

Something snapped. Perhaps it was time to leave this dung heap called earth for good.

"Diaper Boy!"

You're a nobody. You can't even keep a wife satisfied.

A ceaseless tirade in my head continued for days as I drank and remembered.

I carefully spread out a comforter on the sofa, then the plastic shower curtain on top. I placed the next comforter on the plastic and covered myself with another blanket. I had perfectly planned how to check out without leaving a mess for loved ones.

Then, slowly, I placed my service weapon in my mouth, pointing it upward at my brain.

Dad would find me in a day or so — he was coming to visit. The thermostat was on a cool setting, so I probably wouldn't stink. My gunsmith had adjusted the trigger mechanism for "light" pull, and I squeezed the hair trigger — but the pistol seemed *stubborn*. My police weapon was my companion, my savior, my protector, and I knew its action like my own digits.

Why doesn't it fire?

Like a sudden electric shock, a thought lit up my brain: "I forgot to call MOM!" She had made a lot of mistakes in her life, but I owed her a *goodbye*.

I had been awake for 24 hours straight, and I wearily dialed her for our last "chat." But Mom wouldn't let me off the hook for seven hours straight. She wore me plum out, talking. Somehow she sensed my desperation, and

THE ROUGHEST WARD

when I hung up the phone, I just passed out. A man's commanding voice woke me.

"You don't think you have a reason to live, but I am the only reason you are alive."

I scrambled to shake away cobwebs and grabbed my .45.

"Who's in my house? Show yourself!"

A police officer is trained to hunt down a suspect in a building, and I followed protocol — every room and cupboard and closet — and came up dead empty. Every door was still locked, and it began to prickle my neck hairs when I realized that I stood in a supernatural scene: God had saved me and was asserting *who* was really in charge of my life — or death.

Dad arrived the next day.

Virginia:

I'll never date a younger man; I'll never date anyone in law enforcement — especially a cop; I'll never date a guy who's blond ...

I studied Kenny's blond hair and hazel eyes — a *police officer* and younger than I was by years — at a breakfast date. We had danced the previous night at my birthday party, and his openness and honesty had deleted my "nevers" one by one.

At the constable's office, I had barely noticed him; just another uniform needing help with paperwork, a little cocky and jawing with the women at the counter. At my

UNMASKED

birthday party, I took pity on him, all alone, and introduced him around. Our dance was a surprise — as was his attentiveness toward me *and* my feelings for him.

"Hank Williams? Hmmm."

"He's performing at the Summit." He seemed excited and looked even *younger* as he tried to clinch the date while chewing pancakes.

I really had to *think*. Jenn was 11 months old, and I had a pretty stable life, working, caring for my daughter and attending church regularly — and my heart touched God's presence more often lately. I was understanding that Jesus had forgiven all my past, and it changed me! Would a relationship with Kenny threaten my progress? I decided to put the man to the ultimate test.

"I love Hank. Sure, I'll go — *if* you'll go to church with me Sunday." I watched him stop chewing and cogitate for a couple seconds.

"You drive a hard bargain, but, yeah, it's a date."

And Hank was great. The next morning, Kenny picked Jenn and me up for services at my Humble church, all of us dressed to the nines. He savored my daughter's every little move and cry, and my heart began to melt as I watched them together. I worried that I might be falling in love, and it was no secret to me that Kenny's heart was already open to a relationship, too. As the weeks passed, it became harder for us to part company after dates.

Obviously, he had been scarred by his childhood, and his heart still suffered open wounds from religious intolerance. Now he was very wary of trusting church folk

THE ROUGHEST WARD

at all, and I understood completely. Fatherless Jenn had shocked church women I knew, but I was learning that God spoke to me where his people gathered, even if a few were the rude and judgmental.

From Michigan, Kenny called me one night. He was trying to leave his past life behind him and start fresh in his home state, and I had no idea if it was God's will for Jenn and me to be part of his life at all. He sounded sad on the phone.

"If I get this job in Michigan, will you and Jenn come?"

It took me a moment to digest what Kenny was saying. "No, not as your *girlfriend*." My tone was final and a little irritated, and he quickly changed course.

"I wouldn't want you to, Virginia."

Silence.

"Are you asking me to marry you?" His divorce had been finalized only weeks before. What was I getting myself into?

"I dunno. Do you want me to?"

I sighed loudly into the phone. "Kenny, that's got to be your choice..."

Kenny didn't take the job in Michigan. He came back to Houston.

☙☙☙

"You'll both burn in hell if you wed that man!" This was the general consensus among my friends at Humble church. Kenny's divorce (on top of my "Jezebel" past) promised to corrupt their holy atmosphere in the church if we married. We endured their religious haranguing for a time, countering their baseless assertions with some words from the Bible that we learned by reading books like Ed Dobson's *What the Bible Really Says About Marriage, Divorce, and Remarriage*. We also sought counsel from other pastors and finally felt secure that God forgave our past mistakes and would bless our union.

After we married, we found a place to help us rebuild our wrecked spiritual foundations, a Bible study group that we affectionately called Charbroiled-Chicken Bible Study. I was 29, Kenny 24, when he resumed his police patrols in the 5th Ward, and I found myself pregnant with another baby, our first son, whom we named Kenny Martin, III.

Those first years of marriage he battled to keep in custody violent emotions that erupted into accusations and revealed his lack of trust in anyone.

"What time will you be back? Why didn't you call me?"

I felt like one of Kenny's "suspects" under interrogation — all that was missing were my handcuffs. A few months after our second child was born, I discovered that I was pregnant with a son, and I helplessly watched the ugly Houston streets seduce my Kenny, day by day.

With one baby in a highchair and the other in my arms, I struggled to remember the promise God spoke to

THE ROUGHEST WARD

my heart before our wedding: *Virginia, you and your husband will serve me.*

Kenny:

Strangely, the battle to justify our wedding to religious zealots at Humble stirred up yearnings that I believed were long dead. I read Ed Dobson's book with an open Bible at hand to confirm that our vows would be honorable — at least for Virginia's sake — and as I read my little-used Bible, a voice in the depths of my soul invited me to *speak back*.

I tried, but my mind immediately clambered to old bunkers: Every foul response, every hypocrisy, every rejection I had known paraded like a distracting peepshow in my brain.

Christianity in full color! I had experienced *that* in Humble, all over again. My rage, almost comforting in its intimacy, drowned out the voice.

"If *this* is what God is like, I don't need him."

For a time I still attended religious services with Virginia, at a large church where I could feel anonymous. I picked apart every meeting like a crime scene, and in time softball tournaments and other activities replaced church on Sundays and evenings at home with Virginia. I avoided crying babies and dinnertimes, my loving wife and my easy chair — all of which was so alien to my comforting "reality" in the squalid 5th Ward.

Beauty and sweetness in my marriage faded like a Texas sunset; I became darkness inside.

UNMASKED

Yet that d*** "voice" never let up! And it spoke through people.

Aaron, a rookie officer whom I had trained, came off probation and now worked vice, and he hounded me.

"Come to church with us, Kenny."

He knew the dual roles a police officer played: patrolling the cruel streets, then driving home to routines, diapers and a partner *without* a gun — and he somehow handled the quandary with rugged *grace*. He had been irritatingly persistent, and finally I relented.

"Aaron, look, I have a softball tourney this weekend. I'll come *next* Sunday, okay?"

He was beaming in my rearview mirror as I drove off, and I groused a little over giving in to the dogged rookie. The guy was turning out to be a great police officer.

But now he was dead.

I kept my word to Aaron. I stood at the front of his church the next week, studying his lifeless face in the coffin for a few seconds before silently praying, *Oh, God. What have I done? Have I walked away so far that you have forgotten who I am? Did I ever really give my heart to you?*

It had appeared to be a robbery. At an adult bookstore in Houston, Aaron had been writing a ticket to the owner, and a "customer" fired a bullet pointblank into his back. The young man lay on the floor bleeding, pleading for his life, and the perpetrator's second bullet went through his chest, hastening Aaron's soul to Jesus.

Life is fragile.

THE ROUGHEST WARD

At home I helped tuck our two babies in bed, knowing that I had to change my way of thinking if my family was to survive the "mean streets" of everyday living.

"Virginia, I don't even know if I'm a Christian anymore. I feel like I'm heading to hell fast."

My wife had been praying for this day, and the next Sunday we found a little Berean Bible church to attend. Every word the pastor preached seemed like God was speaking to me, and I walked to the front for prayer.

"I don't know if I am saved or not. Or if I meant the words I said as a boy," I told him.

He said simply, "Then do it again."

I poured out my heart to God aloud: I was sorry for my stubbornness, and I asked forgiveness for the constant desire to do the wrong things in my life. I admitted that I had rejected him, and I promised to change course. I asked him to take charge of my mind and heart.

Baptism in water that night sealed the deal in heaven — but not fully in my mind.

Virginia:

The doctor drew a line across Kenny's leg and said, "There's a 90 percent chance that your husband will come out of surgery without about this much." My stomach flipped, and I glanced at Kenny's face. The morphine should have dumbed down his mind by now, but he was wide awake.

"You're NOT cutting off my leg!" It should have been a bellow, but he was too weak from blood loss.

UNMASKED

The doctor nodded an order to the nurse standing by, and she administered more drugs.

"I'll do my best …"

The surgeon was addressing me, but Kenny intercepted the pass. "I don't think you heard me! YOU will NOT cut off my leg!"

I was eight months pregnant with a new baby when Kenny was Life Flighted from a wreck in his patrol car. The doctors did save his leg by pinning him together with rods. I stood in the waiting room, praying, crying, begging that the morphine would take effect. He told me later he felt the drilling in his heel despite anesthesia.

For 35 days, while Kenny lay in traction, I traveled back and forth to the hospital, and when I was home, my babies fussed. My son kicked my ribs, restless to be *out*. Then Kenny came home. Medics wheeled him up the front steps and left me with a laundry list of instructions for his care.

Bones in both ankles and in the balls of Kenny's feet were shattered. His nose had been broken and repaired so he could breathe again, and his chest looked as if it had been beaten with a two-by-four. They said he would never walk again.

Our baby, William, was born five days after Kenny came home — and Kenny reentered the hospital for weeks of treatments when William was 5 days old. During his recovery, Kenny often rejected my tenderness toward him, and I blamed it on the agony he dealt with.

Gradually at home, while I cared for my broken man,

THE ROUGHEST WARD

he seemed to be coming to terms with his new limitations.

Before the accident, Kenny ran five miles a day. He weighed 175 pounds and had single-digit body fat. But after a blood transfusion, his lungs filling with fluid and a host of other health issues, the proud police officer was a husk of his former athletic image. Now he focused on learning to walk again.

In the months that followed, a remarkable healing took place in his body, and his outlook on life seemed brighter at times. He left the wheelchair to learn crutches; he left crutches to use a four-poster cane; then a single cane.

Kenny came back to church and got involved in Sunday school. He sang in the choir, and along with his body, his heart seemed to be healing from boyhood traumas that haunted him most of his life.

But a single upheaval remained for Kenny and me to put behind us. My remaining trust in the man I married shattered like a bullet striking glass, impossible to restore, except by the Creator himself.

Kenny:

Only 11 months after my accident, I was back to work in the 5th Ward. Painful therapy had delivered moderate physical victory over a life sentence of inactivity, and I relearned how to walk.

It was a great day when I strapped on my .45 again and set my cover just right over my brow. My cohorts in blue welcomed me back, and I took a job investigating crime

UNMASKED

scenes — no more jumping fences or hopping car hoods after suspects.

I fell into familiar patterns of thought: Virginia would ultimately leave me. The beautiful brunette I had fallen in love with had vanished in a plump domestic soup of diapers, coloring books and carpooling. I swam in the same chowder myself when I was home, and I couldn't wait to get back to my 5th Ward.

God had wrested away the most cherished part of my police persona — my athletic ability — and now I had to reclaim stature among my peers on a new level. As for my home life: I wanted more — I *deserved* more.

We seldom attended church anymore as a family, but my daughter, Jenn, attended Vacation Bible School at a small church down the street and dragged us to attend a service there.

The pastor's son-in-law was a police officer, and we hit it off right away. All three kids loved the church, and Virginia seemed satisfied, too, so I donned my Sunday best and smiled my way through services. But inside I wasn't smiling.

Self-pity sucked all joy from my life on Monday mornings, and an emotional bond that I should have devoted to my Ginger (Virginia), I squandered on another woman. During the months of my emotional trysts, I still guarded my reputation like my police ID. I feared repercussions if I abandoned Virginia, so instead I did my level best to drive her away.

"When are you going to leave me?"

THE ROUGHEST WARD

I kept up a drumbeat of carefully-chosen, degrading remarks that often included the threat of divorce.

But she wouldn't budge.

Virginia held me in an embrace of unyielding faith that I could not break nor escape. She clung to the promise that we would be serving God together someday and placed me in God's powerful hands to change me.

Then Virginia found out.

Virginia:

My Jekyll-and-Hyde husband suddenly came apart. An avalanche of feelings swept through me when I confronted him with evidence of his infidelity. Did he think I was blind? Phone bills reflecting calls to the same number; night after night away on *business?* He couldn't blame the horrid 5th Ward for his unfaithfulness (even if his trysts *were* only "emotional"), nor could he explain his naked disloyalty. For a time he tried to deny it, but I couldn't let it rest — not if our marriage was to survive.

"We have an appointment with the pastor, Kenny."

His face said more than I could have hoped for.

Shame.

Kenny:

I had become my ex-wife. It doubled me up inside, like a baton to the solar plexus. I knew the pain my Virginia was feeling, because I had been on the receiving end once. I opened up to our pastor about my affair, and my reputation was crushed — not ruined among my police peers, or church folk, or even with my family. My self-respect was ruined for *me*. I saw that my selfishness had nearly lost me the one person in the world who had been loyal. And I recognized Jesus in her devotion. A merciful God had given Virginia the endurance to stay with me, and now it broke my heart: I had caused my wife anguish for nearly as long as we had been married.

I remembered a word, carried in a vision of my little grandmother across my 40 despoiled years: *repentance.* And suddenly I knew exactly what it meant. My heart was broken, and I asked Virginia to forgive me. I asked Jesus to create a clean heart in me and renew a right spirit within me. I made the commitment to change my direction, and this time I *felt* different.

Somehow I sensed a fresh desire to serve God by serving my beloved wife. I felt clean for the first time since I was a child.

༺༻༺༻༺༻

"You know, I think I want to hang up my uniform." The badge on my chest grew heavier each year, like its purpose was finished and it needed to be retired. I wore a sergeant's stripe now, but the climb up the law enforcement ladder held no meaning since I had injected my experiences in the 5th Ward with my faith in Jesus.

At a little local church, I had built a youth group. In my ignorance it shaped up differently from the cookie-cutter Baptist meetings. We went out to talk to people

THE ROUGHEST WARD

about Jesus — even in the 5th Ward! I had never sensed such fulfillment; I felt as if I was moving toward my intended destiny. I loved these kids, I LOVED my own three children and I *adored* my Ginger.

But I didn't love the force anymore. I was a licensed minister now and served as the state rep for peace officers for Christ. I visited hospitals and helped grieving families of slain officers. Internally I was growing in grace (I was learning to forgive people who had abused or hurt me emotionally), and I believed that I should target a life of full-time service to Jesus.

It was time to make a crucial move, and I knew it was God-motivated when Ginger agreed.

Virginia:

My husband packed away his shield from the Houston Police Department with honors, but Kenny will never be free of the 5th Ward. His experiences are imbedded in every word he preaches, every prayer he prays. He has seen the worst of the world and knows that Jesus is the only answer for victims of lust, greed, rage. Jesus is a victim's only hope for true freedom and deliverance.

A few years ago, I helped Kenny renovate old offices for a coffee house, and his God-given vision grew to be a place where hundreds of young people gathered to be loved by Jesus through us.

In his years as a pastor, rugged Kenny-isms have raised a few eyebrows, and I don't expect him to tone down as he grows older:

UNMASKED

"When you're driving through hell, *why, in the hell, stop?*"

"Just because you *were* a victim, you don't have to live a victimized life."

"Don't give credit to God that belongs to the devil."

"If your enemy has a Social Security number and a date of birth, you're fighting the wrong *person*!"

Kenny is preaching on forgiveness again this Sunday. He stands on a stage he built with his own hands, and echoes of his battles resound in the souls of a hundred or more.

"Unforgiveness is like drinking poison and hoping your *enemy* dies!"

And we should know. Kenny and I had to release all the people in our lives from the handcuffs of unforgiveness that bound *us,* and when we did, the weight of the world lifted from our shoulders.

Now we save a special place in our hearts for people crushed by "religion" and longing for a place to know and grow closer to Jesus. We're trusting God to fill our sanctuary with addicts and pimps, prostitutes and law enforcement officers, soccer moms and businessmen — most freed from the slavery of sin — and others, weary victims hungry for their freedom, too.

Kenny and I share the vision, and we are living the challenge — together.

THE HORNET'S NEST
The Story of Bear and Kae Frances
Written by Marty Minchin

My dad first noticed her sitting at the other end of the bar, a tiny thing wearing a white nurse's uniform.

"Look at that girl over there," he said, nudging my shoulder. I turned my head to get a look, and I couldn't take my eyes off her.

I was wearing my dress blues, recently out of the Navy on medical discharge after a mine exploded under our ship in the Gulf of Mexico. The explosion hurt my back, an injury that would haunt me for years. It was 1970, and back home on Long Island, New York, I hadn't found much else to do other than drive my dad to and from the bars at night.

Tonight, Dad was right about the girl. She was really fine, and I wanted to get to know her.

"I'll buy you a drink," I told her, "but first I have to follow my dad home and make sure he gets there safe. I'll be right back."

I was thrilled that she was still at the bar when I returned. She told me she had a beautiful baby girl and was a war widow. We talked for hours. She whooped the tar out of me in a game of pool, but I blame it on all the alcohol I drank that night.

UNMASKED

The next morning, I woke up at home with a terrible headache and a piece of paper in my pocket. All that was written on it was "Kae Frances" and a phone number. I had no memory of meeting a Kae Frances, but I was game for finding out who she was.

Three days later, I met the husband she had lied about not having. I ran him off. Then moved with her and her bright-eyed 1-year-old daughter, Shei Lyn, into a hotel room that was so small, we had to climb over the playpen to get to the bathroom.

I had a stable job, and I desperately wanted my own family. Now I had one.

✧✧✧

My dad came from a very large Polish family of mean alcoholics, and he was no exception. We lived on a dead-end street on Long Island cut in half by a major highway, and everybody on my end knew everybody else. The kids played outside, and nobody locked the doors. The neighbors knew how mean my dad was. They could hear him screaming, and our front yard was the battleground for his yelling fights with my mom.

I was the oldest boy among six children, and my dad beat me every chance he could. If I was in bed when he came home at night, he'd call me downstairs, beat me and send me back to my room. He had hands like iron, and when he hit me, it felt like a hammer slamming into my flesh.

THE HORNET'S NEST

He never smiled. He never once told me he loved me. He mostly ranted and yelled, and my mother stayed out of his way.

The pages of my schoolbooks were sometimes splattered with blood because he hit me on the back of the head so many times, he opened wounds, angry that I couldn't remember the words on the pages. He didn't know it, but the reason I had trouble was because I was dyslexic and couldn't read.

☙☙☙

When I was 9 years old, I found our German across-the-street neighbor, Mr. Muller, sitting in his red Chevrolet pickup truck outside my house. He was wearing his typical baseball cap, work shirt and green khakis, and his leathery skin curved into a smile when he saw me.

"Can I help you?" I asked through the open passenger window.

"Climb in," he said, motioning for me to open the door. "I need some help. Go tell your mom you're going to work."

So I did, and that was the beginning of the happiest part of my childhood.

Mr. Muller owned a dairy farm, and his 36 cows needed to be milked twice daily. He paid me $1 a day, and I worked for him from early in the morning until 10 or 11 at night, seven days a week whenever I could. I'd rather be anywhere than at home with my dad.

UNMASKED

At the farm, I learned how to take care of cows, clean stalls and slaughter animals for meat. I operated tractors and balers, discs and plows, and Mr. Muller taught me how to drive that red truck I loved. At Christmas, he and his wife would give me shoes and clothes for work and school.

Best of all, he told me all the time that I was doing a good job. I soaked up the compliments, because I sure wasn't going to get any at home.

Sometimes Ada, the Mullers' daughter, would take me to the Methodist church on Sundays. I wanted to know God, but it seemed like I could never get to know him personally like she did.

❦❦❦

My dad had a big garden, and he expected all of us to work in it. We never worked side by side in peace because my dad spent most of the time barking orders at us.

After one day of enduring his nonstop hollering and screaming in the garden, I had all I could take.

He raised his hand to strike me, but this time, at 14, I stood up to him.

"If you hit me again, I'm going to take you out," I growled, my fists clenched into balls. I didn't want to hit my dad, but I didn't want to get beat anymore. We both dropped our arms, and I packed a bag and ran away from home.

I lived under a bridge for a while and then stayed with

THE HORNET'S NEST

some friends. Dad finally said he'd change his ways, so I moved back home. But he just channeled his abuse into words instead of beatings.

During that time, Dad did the one good thing he ever did for me. He taught me to be a carpenter, and I had the skills to later build my own house and a lifelong career for myself.

When I got the letter from the Army saying I would be drafted for the Vietnam War, I went straight to the Navy recruiting office and signed up there instead. I was stationed in Panama City, Florida, working on mine sweeps in the Gulf of Mexico.

The explosion under my ship that fateful day threw me to the ground, and the blow was so hard that I couldn't walk for days. The Navy gave me shots of morphine to ease the pain, but the day I was discharged was the day I got my last shot.

I took all kinds of painkillers when I got out, but they didn't seem to work. My personal pain management plan progressed to the point where I easily justified a little reefer here, a little snort there, telling myself it never hurt anybody. It numbed the searing pain in my back, and that's all that mattered.

☙☙☙

When Kae Frances and I married — 24 hours after she divorced her sorry husband and less than two years after we met — I was a drug addict. But she didn't know it. We

UNMASKED

moved into a house around the corner from Kae Frances' grandmother, a spiritual woman who encouraged us to get involved in church. We gave it a half-hearted try, but we rarely attended a Sunday service.

A year later, on Valentine's Day, we had our son, Trey. I had already convinced Kae Frances' ex, who never had any interest in Shei Lyn, to sign papers to let me adopt her. I adored Shei Lyn, who became my sidekick. Kae Frances worked nights, so Shei Lyn and I did everything together. We stayed up late and watched movies, then went out for breakfast in the morning. I loved this life with my family.

The rare times we did go to the church that Kae Frances grew up in, I worried that I was so bad that the huge pipe organ would fall through the floor when I walked through the door. Besides, I was doing well enough on my own, and I didn't feel like I needed God in my life.

Kae Frances finally convinced me to go one Easter Sunday, and I hesitantly took a seat on the pew. When the congregation stood to sing one of the hymns, accompanied by that big pipe organ pounding out the melody, the booming sounds suddenly faded away. I could see people's mouths moving, but there was no noise in that church.

My eyes were drawn to a huge stained-glass window in the front of the church, which seemed to be shining with an unnaturally bright light. The window was a picture of Jesus, who was now filled with light and surrounded by silence except for one clear sound. Jesus' voice was saying, "Look for …"

THE HORNET'S NEST

It freaked me out. The sound swelled around me again as I looked around the church, but I had no idea what those words meant. I spent years trying to figure out what I was supposed to be looking for.

☙☙☙

A few years later, my wife's grandmother and uncle moved to New Mexico. We jumped at the opportunity to move into Grandma's house, not knowing that the house was targeted for previous drug activity. I was readily mistaken for Kae Frances' distant cousin.

"You don't have to do anything," the stranger said. "I need to get this package to Smithtown, and I know Kae Frances works there. Just put it in the backseat, and make sure she leaves the car doors open."

I happily obliged. The drug run was surprisingly easy, as all I had to do was stash the package in Kae Frances' car and convince her not to lock the car doors. She unknowingly became my accomplice. When she went to work the nightshift at Smithtown General Hospital, I'd put the drugs in her car and remind her to leave the car doors unlocked.

When bunches of cash wrapped in newspaper periodically landed on my front lawn in payment, I knew I had found an easy way to support my own expensive drug habit. Even though this cousin was bad news — he and his buddies were in the Mafia — it was a well-paying gig that was easy to hide from my wife.

UNMASKED

We did argue pretty often about why she shouldn't lock the car doors, and I'd blow up at her sometimes when she'd done the laundry without telling me. She washed thousands of dollars of drugs that I'd stashed in my pants cuffs, secret pockets and hemlines.

Construction was slow in the winter months, so I stayed home with the kids and dealt drugs while they napped and Kae Frances worked. But the easy money came to an end when I walked outside one Sunday morning with my cup of coffee. My blood ran cold when I saw Kae Frances' car. The hood was open, and wires jutted out where they had been ripped from the motor.

The "boys," I found out, were very, very upset that Kae Frances had locked her car doors before going into the hospital, and they couldn't get into the car without breaking the windows.

"If this happens again," one of the boys told me, "you won't like what happens to you."

※ ※ ※

When my boss suggested that our construction crew move to Texas, I saw a great opportunity to get out of town where nobody — especially my friends in the Mafia — would know where I was.

"Let's go!" I called out toward my boss' house, the sun rising behind me over Long Island. The boys and I had packed up all of our stuff the night before, and we were there to load him up and get out of town. Kae Frances had

THE HORNET'S NEST

quit her job, and we had rented our house out; we were ready to go.

The boss cracked open his front door and stuck his head out.

"Uh, I forgot to tell you boys, I'm not going after all."

I slowly turned around to face the five guys in my crew, all looking right back at me.

"What are you going to do, Bear?" one of them asked. "Me and the guys don't have jobs anymore."

I didn't have to think twice about an answer. "I'm going to Texas. You boys coming?"

I knew I was going to get myself into a lot of trouble if I stayed.

❧❧❧

We drove out of New York pulling a 22-foot travel trailer with a line of vehicles trailing behind us. We'd park that trailer at night, and Kae Frances and her best friend, who was moving with us, would cook breakfast each morning for all of the guys and hand it to us out the door.

Four days later, our caravan motored through Houston before we found a campground in Magnolia, a town just north of the big city. The girls stayed there during the day while the guys looked for work.

We had a hard time finding a footing in Texas. Sometimes contractors would rip us off, and my crew would end up with $5 for a day's work.

Finally, a general contractor saw my crew's talent. We

UNMASKED

became known as the "Hit and Run Crew" because we could put up all the 2-inch woodwork for a 1,600-square-foot house in eight hours. A bare lot in the morning — when we left at night, a house frame would be standing.

I soon got a job as a general contractor myself, working for a company. I directed a 53-man crew, and Kae Frances handled the paperwork. Being in charge meant I didn't have to work as much, giving me plenty of time to buy and sell drugs. Making up excuses to Kae Frances became a major past time. When I had to explain why yet another weirdo was sitting on our front porch when we came home from the movies, I always told her it was something about a job.

My appearances at home became rare. My kids would make snide remarks like, "Is that our daddy?" when I did grace the doorway.

I was turning into my father, mean and aggressive. I carried a shotgun named Davy, after Davy Crockett, and I readily used it to threaten anyone who owed me money. The arguments with Kae Frances about the laundry escalated, but she just figured it was because I came from an angry home.

ථ⊸ථ⊸ථ⊸

Drugs make you do stupid things, even using your own children to support your habit.

In 1980, I had made enough money to buy a little ranch in Magnolia and stock it with animals. Shei Lyn

THE HORNET'S NEST

loved animals, and we filled our ranch with cows, chickens, horses and pigs.

Shei Lyn helped me grow plants from seed, and together we planted a crop of healthy marijuana trees in the backyard. She would water those plants every night, and when I asked, she would till a little cow manure in the ground around them.

When she wondered what they were, I told her they were odd-looking plants, and I liked them.

༻✦༺

Kae Frances had mostly stayed away from drugs, and by now she knew I was selling and using. She never smoked herself, but if a bunch of us were in the van, she couldn't help getting high from the smoke from everybody else's joints. But one night on the porch swing, her curiosity got the best of her.

"I'd like to take a toke of something myself," she said.

Now, I didn't ever force Kae Frances into anything. Drugs take you somewhere you don't want to go and will make you do things you're not proud of. But that night, I rolled a joint just for her.

She got a little hazy after a couple of tokes, so I helped her to bed, stretched her arms down by her side and tucked the blankets around her really tight. I thought she was going to sleep, so I never did loosen those blankets.

Kae Frances, though, woke up feeling paralyzed, and she couldn't move or talk. She said she felt like she was in a coffin, and she was so scared that after that night she stayed away from drugs for good.

❧❧❧

Afraid that the people I worked with knew a little too much about my using and dealing drugs, I took a new job with a cabinet company that was five hours away.

"I'm fixin' to leave," I called out to Kae Frances one morning after I'd packed my truck. I kissed her and my two sweet children goodbye, told Kae Frances I loved her and drove off into the dry Texas landscape. My weekday home would now be a barren motel room.

Usually after work, I'd do some drugs in my room and go to sleep. One night, though, the guys gathered in the parking lot and asked me to come out and have some barbecue.

We stood around outside smoking weed, the tiny lights from the ends of our joints shining in the twilight. The conversation went round and round, always about drugs. And when I met a woman at the party that night, drugs were all that were on my mind. She had a sizeable stash, she promised, and I readily followed her back to her place around the corner to check it out.

She pushed the door open, motioning to a trunk in the living room.

"This is what you wanted to see," she said, clicking on the lights before slowly opening the lid. My eyes widened as I took in the trunk's contents. It was unbelievable.

THE HORNET'S NEST

Color after color, packages, pills, needles, bottles, every kind of drug imaginable. There was cocaine, crack, pills and at least 10 pounds of weed. I felt like a fat kid in a candy store.

This was life changing. It only took a moment for me to decide that *this* was what I wanted. These drugs. And this woman who would give them to me.

I didn't want my family anymore, or at least that's what I told them. Kae Frances' heart broke when I announced that I didn't love her and never had, the lies flowing off my lips before I had a chance to think about what I was saying. I did tell my children that I loved them but that I had to go. I abandoned Kae Frances, our ranch, our family and our life to move in with a stranger and her smorgasbord of drugs.

The woman gave me full access to the trunk, and I stayed in a stupor for days and days, drifting along in such a haze that I couldn't even figure out what day it was, much less what I had done to my wife and children.

☙☙☙

While I was gone, Kae Frances came to one of the lowest points in her life and cried out to God for help. She accepted Jesus in her heart and became a Christian.

She had cried and cried after I left, so much that when she was finally empty of tears, she was filled up with God. If a church in town was holding a service, she and the kids were there. The Bible stories she'd heard all her life came alive, and Kae Frances was suddenly so passionate about God that she was freaking out her patients and co-workers. When it was suggested that she quit her job, she did. She was so high on her relationship with God that she didn't care.

And when Trey had a vision during a Peewee football game, it didn't much surprise Kae Frances.

The kids were squared up on the line of scrimmage, helmet to helmet, staring each other down before the snap. Suddenly, Trey jumped up and ran off the field in tears, crying out for his mom. "Daddy's going to die," he sobbed. "I saw Daddy, and he was in the hospital. He had a heart attack, and he's going to die."

Kae Frances had no idea what was happening, but she believed that God had given Trey the vision as a warning of what was about to happen. She and Trey prayed right there, and when they said "amen," they knew in their hearts that I may be in the hospital, but that I was okay.

The next day a phone call confirmed the vision, so Trey and Kae Frances drove the three hours to the hospital.

☙☙☙

I saw Kae Frances and Trey in the hospital room, but I wasn't in my right mind. I had done so many drugs that I had suffered a nervous breakdown.

The room seemed to be under water, with everyone moving and talking in slow motion. The woman was

THE HORNET'S NEST

there, and for some reason, Kae Frances hugged her. "Take care of him," she said and then added under her breath, "until I get him back."

I felt tears on my face as I thought about the mess I had gotten myself into. I wanted to go home with Kae Frances and Trey, but I was shaky and scared at the ugliness of what I had done to her and afraid to talk to her about coming back. I was so, so sorry, and if my wife had just asked me to come home with her, I would have jumped up and went.

She didn't ask.

Kae Frances and Trey walked out, leaving me there with the woman. They didn't know what the future would hold other than, with certainty from God, I wasn't going to die.

❧❧❧

When I recovered, the woman and I moved to California. I got a part-time job and fell right back into buying and selling drugs. Work wasn't that appealing, so we organized a huge bash on a mountainside near San Bernardino. This epic party would last for days, fueled by drugs and alcohol.

When Kae Frances got home, she and her friend started to pray for me. Specifically, they prayed that I'd come home. Instead of things getting better, I had moved even farther away … all the way up Kimbark Mountain in California. Eventually the Bible verse Exodus 23:28

UNMASKED

seemed to fit, and they prayed to God about it: "I will send the hornet ahead of you to drive the Hivites, Canaanites and Hittites out of your way."

Kae Frances saw those tribe names in that verse as representing the enemy that had taken me away. She knew for sure that God had given me to her, and she was going to pray me back home.

She wanted me off the mountain and in Magnolia, even if it took a swarm of Biblical hornets to get me back!

❦❦❦

We set up camp on the mountain on a cool California morning, and car after car followed behind us, full of people who filled our campsite. Someone lit a huge bonfire in the center of the party, and all around us people drank, smoked and did drugs. Alcohol was my choice that day.

I stored part of my stock in my truck, and at one point I wandered over to fetch the fifth of Old Grand-Dad out of my glove compartment and the case of beer that was on ice in the toolbox. Not too eager to rejoin the party, I settled into the driver's seat, took a swig out of my bottle and reached over for a beer, feeling satisfied with the massive bash outside.

A weird buzzing sound outside interrupted my drunken relaxation.

Through the windshield I saw that the air was thick with black swarming insects that looked like bees. A huge

THE HORNET'S NEST

cloud of buzzing bugs was headed right for me, and my truck windows were open. A few slipped into the cab as I frantically rolled up the windows and jammed the key into the ignition.

I took off down the mountain, driving through a screaming, hollering crowd running in the same direction. They grabbed the door handles, trying to get into the safety of the cab, but I pushed the accelerator a little harder and locked the doors. No way was I going to stop for any of these people.

I left everyone there, including the woman. All I wanted was to get off that mountain and away from those bees.

When I got to the base, far ahead of the runners and the insects, I felt like a lot of things had been lifted off my mind. Life, for the moment, seemed a little clearer.

Maybe, I thought, *I'll call home and see how the kids are doing.*

"I'm getting tired," I told Kae Frances. "I just want to come home and see the kids for a little bit."

I got in my truck and drove for three days, working through most of the beer, the Old Grand-Dad and the three packs of reefers in my truck along the way. As I neared Magnolia, the sun rising over the horizon, I hummed along to one of my favorite songs, "Tie a Yellow Ribbon Round the Old Oak Tree," when it came on the radio.

I pulled up at the ranch early Easter Sunday morning. Wouldn't you know, anticipating my return, Kae Frances had tied yellow ribbons around at least 40 oak trees in our front yard!

When she and the kids walked outside to meet me, it felt like nothing had changed, like I was coming up the driveway after a day at work.

☙☙☙

It felt good to be home, so good that Kae Frances easily talked me into going to church with her that morning; I would have done anything to stick around a little longer. I was now seeing Kae Frances and the kids with a clear head, and I realized what I was losing.

My old life seemed to be waiting for me inside the house. My place at the table was set, and my clothes in my dresser drawers. Trey and Shei Lyn jumped around in excitement because we were going to church as a family of four.

Church didn't do much for me that morning. Everywhere I looked, I felt bad. Five or six boys I used to sell drugs to sat in pews ahead of us with their wives, and I thought about how I ruined all of these lives. I felt so dirty that I couldn't even look at Kae Frances half the time.

"Why don't you stay for a couple of days?" Kae Frances asked when we got home. I agreed to it.

"Let's get whatever you have out of the truck and clean it out," she said. "You've had a long trip."

I headed straight to the glove compartment to finish off the last of the bourbon. My reefer was gone, and I had

THE HORNET'S NEST

only a couple of beers left in the toolbox. I needed to get to a store to replenish my supply, but I couldn't leave. My kids danced around, saying, "Daddy's home!" over and over, and I didn't want to leave them quite yet, even for a few minutes.

"What is this?" Kae Frances demanded, backing out of the cab of the truck and holding out her hand, palm up.

I grabbed her hand and examined the dead bug on it.

"That's a hornet," I told her.

"Where did it come from?" Her voice pitched higher and louder. "Are you sure it's a hornet?"

"Yes, ma'am," I replied, wondering why she was making such a big deal over a dead bug in a truck. "I know hornets, wasps, bees, yellow jackets. It's a hornet all right. I just don't know how it got in the truck because I thought I got rid of them all."

"What do you mean?" Kae Frances asked slowly, her eyes boring into me.

"We were having a party, and it seemed like this herd of bees came from nowhere …"

Any more details of my story were lost because Kae Frances had turned into a screaming, dancing fool. I know even the neighbors heard her yelling and praising the Lord, and I couldn't for the life of me figure out what was going on.

I finally got her calmed down enough to explain.

She told me she and our neighbor had been praying that God would send a swarm of hornets to run me off a mountain and right back home.

UNMASKED

"I knew that God was going to bring you back. Period. End of story," she said, tears shining in her eyes. "I just didn't know when or how it would happen."

"You really believe that stuff, huh?" I asked her. She nodded enthusiastically. "Well, God hasn't made a believer out of me because I don't see it myself."

☙☙☙

I woke up at 2 a.m. sweating and shaking like a leaf. The sheets were soaked. Kae Frances had invited me to sleep in our bed, and I had found some pajamas right where they belonged in the dresser.

The pain was sweeping through my back. I hadn't drunk or smoked anything since the afternoon before.

"Kae Frances, I've got to have something now," I whispered.

"I'll go to the kitchen and see what I have." She returned with a water glass filled with bourbon.

"I don't even know where this came from," she said, putting the glass into my trembling hands. Her willingness to serve me alcohol surprised me, but I was so happy to see that drink that I didn't care where it had come from.

"Do you mind if I pray for you?" Kae Frances asked.

"As long as you don't stop me from drinking."

She started praying, and I tipped that glass to my mouth and started drinking. With that first mouthful of fiery liquid, I could feel my body relax.

I drank and drank while Kae Frances prayed, and

THE HORNET'S NEST

when the glass was empty, I looked over at Kae Frances and hardly recognized her.

She was standing on the bed, an angel in white, praying in a language I didn't understand.

Maybe I'm really messed up tonight, but I don't care. I got what I wanted.

☙☙☙

On a normal morning, I would wake up, hit the alarm off and unscrew the bottle by my bed. I'd usually take a few drinks before my feet were firm on the floor, and then I'd go outside to cough.

My lungs were terrible from the years of smoking cigarettes, and it was exhausting to start every day practically hacking up a lung. Every winter, without fail, I got at least one case of pneumonia.

The day after Kae Frances prayed, I woke up to a rich coffee smell floating through the house. Instead of reaching for a bottle, I walked into the kitchen and enjoyed a cup of coffee with my wife.

Kae Frances' prayers had delivered me from alcohol. That day, I started a new life, and I never touched alcohol again. God was trying to show himself to me.

Yet, I wasn't quite ready for him.

☙☙☙

My few days at home stretched out into months. The neighbors who had prayed the hornet prayer with Kae

UNMASKED

Frances invited us to their church for a remarriage ceremony, and we renewed our vows.

An altar call followed, and Kae Frances went forward because she wanted the pastor to pray for her eyes. She was born cross-eyed; doctors overcorrected during surgery, and one eye looked up and one out. It had been a lifelong insecurity for her.

I wanted God to help Kae Frances with her eyes, so I slid out of the pew and followed her to the front of the church. I prayed so hard, begging God to do whatever he could for her. My prayers were so intense that I slipped into another language; a special prayer language that I didn't even know was possible. God filled me with the Holy Spirit that night, and I prayed for almost an hour, even though it seemed like only 30 seconds to me.

After that night, I started to get serious about God. He'd delivered me from alcohol and filled me with his Spirit, but I hadn't let go of the drugs and cigarettes.

It was time for me to give up smoking, but I needed God's help.

సౌసౌసౌ

Kae Frances and I had decided to move back to New York so that our children could get to know their grandparents. When the girl who offered to buy our house in Magnolia backed out at the last minute, we ended up spending our last days in Texas in a freezing, empty house with hardly any furniture.

THE HORNET'S NEST

We pushed blankets against the doors and windows to keep out the cold and camped out in the living room. We cooked on a Ben Franklin stove and listened to the radio, our only form of entertainment. One day, that radio delivered the message that would be the answer to my prayers about cigarettes.

A country church was holding a healing and deliverance service that night. I decided that I needed to go, and I needed to be the first in line for prayer.

"If I don't go and get prayed for first, it's not going to happen," I told my family as we wrestled around on the living room floor. "I need all the power that boy's got."

Trey jumped on the back of my neck. "Dad, you don't have to be first."

I pulled him around to face me. "Yes, I do." I was a big man, and it was going to take a lot of power to pray the desire for cigarettes out of me.

That evening, I set my cigarettes and 24-karat gold Zippo lighter on the coffee table in the living room, because if I was going to be delivered, I wouldn't need them anymore. Kae Frances and I climbed into the truck and headed out to pick up my buddy, who also smoked and who wanted to attend the service.

It was chaos at his house. He wasn't ready, his kids were running around everywhere and we were very late. He was sure he knew where the church was, but we ended up in a cow pasture. Luckily the church was just around the corner in another cow pasture; we had to pick our way around cow patties to get to the door.

UNMASKED

My heart sank when we reached the building. The church was so packed that the only seats left were chairs lined up along the back wall. I could hardly see the stage, which was at least 50 feet wide. The pastor looked like an ant standing on it.

This is no way to treat somebody who's here to get his healing first, I fumed to myself. I folded my arms, and between my attitude and the big chip on my shoulder, my frustration was clear.

Somehow the pastor got onto a tirade about versions of the Bible.

"Anybody who reads a Living Bible isn't reading a REAL Bible," he preached. Well, I had a Living Bible translation right there in my lap. (It was actually the first book I was able to read.) I threw that Bible on the concrete floor. *Thwack!* It echoed through the building.

"I ain't reading this no more," I announced.

The service went on in spite of my temper tantrum, which the pastor probably didn't notice, and before he could even begin the altar call, people were tossing cigarettes and lighters at him. My anger burned hotter because I had left mine at home. *How am I supposed to be delivered from stuff I didn't even have with me?*

When I looked up, the pastor had walked into the crowd and was engulfed in the hundreds of people wanting to be near him. I couldn't even see the stage anymore.

"It's not my time," I told Kae Frances. "I'm not going to go. If I can't be first, I'm not going."

THE HORNET'S NEST

"Oh, yes, you are." Kae Frances had no intention of leaving.

"Oh, no, I'm not."

The music stopped, the sudden silence ending our squabble. It was so quiet I thought someone had gotten hurt.

The pastor climbed back on stage and grabbed his microphone.

"When God tells you to do something, you just got to do it," he announced. "God told me just now, standing right down there in the crowd, that I got to pray for some man first."

That got my attention.

"I don't know who this guy is, but God told me you and him got a lot in common. You're both carpenters. I don't have enough power to deliver you from what it is you need deliverance from. There's something to do with wood, and that's your bond.

"I need some wood!" he called out, and the drummer from the praise band leapt up and offered the pastor his wooden drumsticks.

"I'm going to break them." The pastor held the drumsticks above his head and somehow snapped them in two. Then he pointed at me, way back in the crowd.

"Sir, God wants me to pray for you first."

That's when I knew God was real. My wife saw all of this happen. She heard me telling everybody I had to be first. I couldn't see that pastor, yet he picked me out of a crowd.

UNMASKED

We wove through the crowd to the front, and when that pastor laid his hand on me and started praying, a warmth came over me that seemed to rub me all over inside, scrubbing my lungs and my heart. I was so thankful, and I felt certain I was healed that night.

We had a great discussion with the pastor after the service, and I got a new Bible. I never coughed again or got pneumonia, and that lighter and cigarettes sat on the coffee table until we moved.

We threw it all away on the way out the door.

৵৵৵

We lasted three months in New York.

We had become laidback Texans, which didn't mesh well with our New York family. Everything was expensive, and when a deal to buy a piece of property fell through, we headed back west, stopping in Louisiana where some old drug buddies of mine lived. We stayed for three years.

While God had delivered me from cigarettes and alcohol, I still had back pain and took drugs to alleviate it.

After two years, I found a job back in Texas. Kae Frances decided to stay in Louisiana for one more year so that Shei Lyn could finish high school. The day after Shei Lyn's graduation, Kae Frances and the kids packed the car to join me in Texas.

I had moved back into the same mobile home where my weird drug acquaintances used to wait on the front porch, and after a year as a bachelor, I had become

THE HORNET'S NEST

accustomed to living by myself. My old friends had stirred up all kinds of lies and trouble, and when Kae Frances arrived, it was like she had stepped on another hornet's nest. It put a terrible strain on our marriage.

Finally, Kae Frances had enough.

"Devil!" she screamed one afternoon, looking straight at me. "Get out of this house!"

Apparently, she was actually tired of the devil wreaking havoc in our home, but at the time, I didn't know that. I thought she wanted *me* to move out. So I did. I moved in with my sister, who lived by the beach in Florida.

It was so easy to slip back into the drug scene there. I was unhappy and depressed, not doing much of anything. On most nights, I sat out by the water by myself, looking out into the black of night and thinking about what had happened to my life. The steady sounds of the ocean's waves were somehow soothing.

God? Why would you bring me all this way to let me fall all the way into it again?

A calm voice rolled in with the waves. *I didn't bring you anywhere. I'm still right here by your side. You're the one who walked away.*

Tears poured from my eyes, and I cried and carried on all by myself on that beach.

Take me back, I begged God.

I never let you go.

By the time I got up off the sand and brushed off my clothes, I had a different relationship with God, a new understanding of what he expects from us. It had been several months since I'd left Kae Frances for the second time, and I wanted to go home.

She let me move back in, saying there was something different about me. And there was a lot different about our lives.

While I was gone, Shei Lyn had gotten pregnant by her girlfriend's brother, and I was about to become a grandfather.

꙳꙳꙳

This time, I stayed out of the drug scene. I had been healed of back pain at a miraculous prayer service in Louisiana, and now I spent my time working and volunteering in the community garden. When people and pastors stopped to talk to me, it felt good that people paid attention to me for something other than drugs. We joined Upper Room Fellowship in 2006, quickly connecting with our pastor, PK, and his wife, Virginia.

When that call came at work one morning, it changed everything. I needed our church family more than ever.

My teenage granddaughter was screaming so hysterically that I could hardly understand her.

"Papaw, she's dead, she's dead!"

"Now, don't be playing with me like that." *Why would my granddaughter call me like this at work?*

"Papaw, she's cold. She won't wake up."

I believed her then. I called 911 and drove over to Shei

THE HORNET'S NEST

Lyn's house as fast as I could, where I found two skinny kids crying because they'd lost their mother due to two prescribed medications that didn't mix. Shei Lyn had gone to sleep the night before. She never woke up.

I had lost my precious daughter, who I'd loved since I met her on my first date with Kae Frances. We found Shei Lyn on the sofa with her Bible next to her. She had rededicated her life to Christ just a week before, and she died as a child of God.

PK and Virginia stayed with us almost constantly for the next few days as we sorted through our own devastation and the logistics of Shei Lyn's life. PK is a former Houston police officer, and he arrived at Shei Lyn's house not long after I did, knowing what questions to ask and how to handle the situation. The church showered us with food, gifts and cards, treating us better than I've treated people I've known for years and years. It's just amazing that our church family supported us the way they did.

※ ※ ※

The blow of Shei Lyn's death was followed by another round of troubled times, and for the first few years, the life we had gotten on track was stirred up again like a nest of hornets. The grandkids, Mariah Nicole and her brother, Eddie, moved in with us. Kae Frances and I were suddenly parents to two young, undisciplined teenagers.

The kids slept in donated bunk beds in our small guest

room, and eventually I added onto my house and built them each their own bedroom. Mariah Nicole's room is decked out in everything cheerleading, and Eddie has a football room. Neither had ever had a room to themselves.

The grandkids' rebellious activities were stressful. Previous to Shei Lyn's death, Mariah Nicole had been in trouble at school for drugs, and soon after Eddie was hauled out of school for drug involvement as well. Both spent time in juvenile detention. Sam, Shei Lyn's oldest, has also served jail time. But this time served as a turning point for each of them, and God ministered and answered prayers.

These days, when I move to get out of my chair, Eddie often appears in front of me and grabs my hands.

"Let me help you, Papaw," and I let him pull me up. If I'm working in the yard, he'll take over, telling me he likes to sweat and wants to do the work.

By that time, I may have gotten a whiff of something baking in the kitchen, where Mariah Nicole's probably cooking a dessert for me.

These two children are now more thankful and take better care of me and Kae Frances than I could have ever imagined. God asked us to take care of these children, and because of our obedience, God has brought peace to our family.

Those hornets have flown away.

SMALL TOWN TALES
The Story of Mariah Nicole
Written by Karen Koczwara

Something was terribly wrong with my mother. I knew it in my gut as I bent over and shook her, gently at first, and then harder. "Mom, wake up!" I cried, a lump forming in my throat. "Wake up!"

My mother's thick sandy-blond hair curled around her face in wisps as she lay on the couch, her arms dangling limply at her side. I grabbed her wrist and felt for a pulse, for a sign of life that would relieve the adrenaline racing through my blood. But there was nothing.

"Mom, please!" Tears welled in my eyes as I frantically shook her again, half expecting her to jump up, open her green eyes and flash me a reassuring smile. "Help, someone, help!" I screamed.

My mother's friend flew into the room, pulled her off the couch and began to administer CPR. The room spun around me as I stood there helplessly, taking in the scene like a spectator at a bad horror movie. *Please, God, don't let this be happening...*

"What's going on?" My brother Eddie raced to my side. "What's wrong with Mom?" he cried, his eyes wide with alarm.

"She's not breathing! I don't know ... I don't know ..." My words tumbled out as I tried to catch my breath.

UNMASKED

"Mom!" Eddie knelt over my mother, shaking her, looking for any sign of life. "Wake up, Mom!"

God, please, not my mother, not now! My mind flashed to my father, lying in a hospital bed a few miles from here, fighting for his life. We'd already been through so much ... first Dad, and now my mother, too? *God, don't take them both!*

☙☙☙

Magnolia, Texas, is the sort of town one might blink and miss as they pass through on a leisurely Sunday drive. Located just outside of Houston, Texas, it boasts of sprawling horse properties, acres of green grass, picturesque brick houses and tall, thick trees. Some might call it suburbia, the perfect place to raise a family. Magnolia is where my story begins; it is behind the doors of one of those little brick houses that my tragedy unfolds.

My mother, Shei Lyn, birthed me in 1993. My brother Eddie came along just 16 months later; we were inseparable from birth. My mother always dressed us the same when we were toddlers, prompting many folks to stop and ask if we were twins. "Why, yes, they are!" my mother sometimes replied with a smile, rumpling our matching blond hair.

With her thick curly blond hair and green eyes that turned ice blue the second she grew mad, my mother was the no-nonsense practical type. Born in New York, she later moved to Texas with her family and settled onto a

SMALL TOWN TALES

farm, where she spent her days riding horses and hunting with her younger brother. Late in her teen years, she stumbled into the arms of the wrong guy and wound up pregnant with my older brother, Sam; the relationship with his father soon fizzled. My grandfather introduced my mother to my father when Sam was a toddler, and my mother fell in love with the fair-skinned, dark-haired man. They rented a little house in Magnolia, and I came along a couple years later. Eddie was 2 when my parents finally married. My mother hoped we'd now be the perfect family, but the rest of our story was anything but a fairytale.

"Where you goin'?" I asked my older brother one afternoon as he tromped down the front steps.

"Just out with my friends," he called back. "Be back later!"

"Can I come?" I trotted after him, my tiny legs no match for his longer ones. "Please?" At 5 years old, I looked up to Sam and wanted to do whatever he was doing, whether digging in the dirt or riding bikes through the mud.

"Not this time, Sis," he replied with an apologetic smile. "Sorry."

I plopped onto the porch steps and sighed. These days, my father wasn't around much. He often disappeared late at night and was nowhere to be found in the morning. My mother said he had business to take care of, that he would be back soon.

UNMASKED

But her weary eyes told me there was more to the story.

I started school and enjoyed making new friends. Sam was making new friends, too. One day, I followed him to a friend's house, where he pulled out a strange-looking cigarette. "What's that?" I asked, leaning in with curiosity as he lit one end of it and took a deep breath.

"Just weed," he replied, exhaling casually. "You're only 6; you're too young to try it, Sis."

"Aw, come on," I pressed, sticking out my bottom lip. "Lemme try."

"All right, one hit, okay?" He handed the cigarette to me and watched as I put it awkwardly to my lips and inhaled as I'd seen him do. The smoke burned my lungs, and I began to cough uncontrollably. Wanting to impress Sam, I took another hit and tried to suppress the next round of coughs. My head felt light and funny, and I suddenly needed to sit down.

"See, told ya you wouldn't like it," Sam teased, snatching the joint back from me.

"Who said I didn't like it?" I leaned back in my chair as the room spun around me in a blur of fuzzy colors. The burning sensation had now worked its way down to my stomach, and I felt like I might throw up. That was definitely one strong cigarette!

My father's absences grew more frequent.

"He's doing business again. He'll be home soon," my mother said vaguely when I persistently asked about his whereabouts.

SMALL TOWN TALES

She worked long days in the office at her father's hydraulics parts shop and was often too tired to do much when she came home and kicked off her shoes. "Can you come over and rub my back for a minute?" she asked, sinking onto the couch. My mother explained that her back hurt her very much because she'd ruptured two discs. When I asked if that was why she needed all the pills in that little orange bottle, she nodded wearily.

I stopped asking about my father's frequent disappearances after a while and retreated to smoking "weed" with my brother and his friends. Eventually, it stopped burning my lungs, but the pit in my stomach only grew worse as the tension mounted in our home.

☙☙☙

Riding horses was one of the bright spots of my childhood. I loved nothing more than mounting a horse and feeling the wind in my hair as the creature clomped along at a leisurely pace. On that horse, I forgot all about my father's disappearances, my mother's sad, brave smile and the yelling that I sometimes overheard in the kitchen late at night.

"We should sign you up for competition," my mother said one day as I hopped off my horse. "What would you think about that?"

My eyes lit up. I'd been around horses nearly all my life, but riding competitively was a much different story than riding for fun. "Yeah, let's do it!" I agreed eagerly.

UNMASKED

Secretly, I hoped it meant more time for my mother and I to bond.

I kept busy riding horses that year and also dabbled with cheerleading. Eddie joined the football team at school. He was a natural athlete, alternating between fullback and linebacker positions. We attended every one of his games, cheering from the sidelines as he charged down the field with the ball. Sometimes, my father showed up, too, and for a brief moment, we looked like the average all-American family in the stands.

I kept smoking pot with my brother, but the high I got from a joint now didn't seem strong enough. When I was 11 years old, I snuck a few pills from that little orange bottle in my mother's purse and slipped them in my pocket. Later that night, I downed them with a tall glass of water and waited for them to kick in. To my pleasant surprise, they relaxed my body, and for a few moments, all of my troubles disappeared.

I soon learned OxyContin was the new "crack" at my new junior high. Looking for a quick way to make a few bucks, I snuck a few more pills and brought them to school with me one day. "You sure she's gonna pay up for these?" I asked my friend as I slipped the pills into her hands between classes.

"Of course," my friend assured me. "I'll have your cash by the end of the day."

As promised, my friend returned that afternoon with a small wad of cash. I shoved it in my pocket and smiled. *Boy, that was easy!*

SMALL TOWN TALES

Perhaps I could find a few more customers around campus.

As the weeks passed, I fell into a steady routine. While my mother slept, I snuck a few more pills from her purse and sold them to my peers at school the next day. *She'll never notice,* I reassured myself. The money was adding up nicely; I might never need to work in fast food if I kept this up.

My grandparents, known to others as Bear and Kae Frances, lived just a few miles away, and I enjoyed spending time at their house. My grandmother often talked about God and took me to church. I loved learning about a God who loved me so much; it was a great comfort to know that, despite my earthly father's frequent absences, I had a heavenly father who would never let me down. Church was yet another welcome refuge from my troubled home. By now, I had learned the truth. My father had a serious drug problem; trips to a crack house in Houston explained his late-night disappearances. I didn't know much about drugs, but I did know they did bad things to people's bodies and to their families. And my family was suffering more than ever.

One night, I awoke to find Sam missing from his bed. I padded down the hall to my mother's room and found her sleeping on the rumpled covers alone. "Where's Sam?" I whispered, shaking her.

My mother rubbed her eyes groggily and slowly sat up. "What do you mean?" she croaked.

UNMASKED

"He's gone! So's Dad!"

"If he took him where I think he did …" My mother's voice trailed off as her green eyes turned icy blue with anger. "Go back to bed, Mariah Nicole. I'll deal with this."

"But what if something happens to him?" I cried, horrible images filling my mind. Sam was older than me, but he was still just a kid. How dare my dad drag him out with him!

I slept fitfully that night, tossing and turning until the sun peeked its way through my bedroom window. I awoke to harsh voices down the hall; my mother's was shrill, my father's angrier than I'd heard in some time. "Just stay out of it, okay?" he hollered. "Sam's a big kid!"

"But he's my son!" my mother yelled back.

The screaming continued all morning. When at last it subsided, I dragged myself out of bed and found my mother in tears as she yanked on her work clothes. "Is Sam okay?" I dared to ask.

"He's fine," she mumbled. "He's gone back to bed. You should get ready for school, Mariah."

I took a deep breath. "Why don't you leave Dad?" I was old enough to know what divorce was. Grandma said God didn't like it, but I wondered if God had ever dealt with a crack addict.

My mother sighed as she slipped into her heels. "I love him, Mariah. It's just … complicated. Your father is trying, and I'm sure things will get better in the future. Now go on and get your breakfast."

I headed off to school, relieved to have yet another

place to escape to. A's came easily for me, and teachers always adored me. The moment I slipped into my desk, I tried to forget the chaos at home and focus on my studies.

"Mariah, if you have time next week, I'd love your help on a project I'm working on," one of my teachers requested.

"Sure!" I replied eagerly. "Just let me know how I can help." Little did she know that her model student was trying to hold up a crumbling house on the other side of town.

I developed migraines as I got older, sometimes so debilitating that they forced me to stay home from school. As my head pounded in pain, a steady ache grew in my heart as well. The teeny glimmer of hope in my mother's eyes made me want to believe my father would change as well, but his behavior had only grown more erratic. He stole from a convenience store and was sentenced to jail time. From there, he spent time in rehab, where he swore he'd get his act together once and for all.

"This won't happen again," my father assured us. "I promise you all, this is the last time. I'm so sorry. I'm done with the drugs."

My brothers, mother and I all nodded our heads, but our insides argued with the man who had let us down repeatedly. We knew better; the "last time" was never the last.

One morning, I wandered into the kitchen to find my mother making sandwiches. "What are those for?" I asked.

"We're taking them to your father at the rehab center,"

UNMASKED

she replied, forcing a smile. "They're having a family get-together down there, and we're going to all show up. It will mean a lot to him to have us there."

I watched her glob the mayonnaise on the bread and felt my heart sink. What hope was she still holding onto? We all knew the drill by now. The minute Dad got out, he'd go right back to his ways and disappear off to those crack houses in Houston again or go rip off some convenience store. I was tired of wishing things would change.

We showed up at my father's function and found him mingling with some guys. "I brought you your favorite lunch," my mother said, proudly pulling a sandwich out of her bag. "Hope you like it."

My father picked up the sandwich, took one bite and promptly threw it at her. "This is nasty! Why can't you do anything right?" he screamed. "You know I don't like mayo!"

My mother recoiled in disappointment. "I'm sorry," she faltered. "I thought you did."

"You should know better, you really should." My father lunged for her car keys, grabbed them out of her hands and stormed off.

I stood there, watching my mother fight back angry tears as she held the half-eaten sandwich in her hands. "I thought he liked mayonnaise," she mumbled.

"Mom, he's got our keys. Let's get out of here," I said, jumping into take-charge mode. I wanted nothing more to do with my father's disrespectful behavior.

SMALL TOWN TALES

We raced all over the place, searching for the keys. With each ticking minute, I grew angrier. How could he do this to our family, to my mother, who was trying so hard to hold it together? When would the madness end?

At last, my mother found the car keys, and we drove home in silence, each in our own world of hurt. I stared out the window at the vast blue Texas sky and wondered if maybe there was a better life somewhere on the other side of those big puffy clouds.

Eddie's football games were one of the few things that united us as a family. My mother and I never missed a game, always cheering our own superstar from the sidelines as he raced down the field. One evening during a game, Eddie got tackled and crumpled to the ground. When he didn't get up after the expected few seconds, my sisterly instincts and a surge of adrenaline kicked in. I jumped out of my seat and ran toward the field, where a sea of coaches and trainers surrounded my brother.

"Is he okay?" I cried, riddled with panic. Eddie was my rock; if anyone dared pick on me at school, he was the first to defend me. He was the one I shared my deepest secrets and heartaches with; if anything happened to my brother, a piece of me would die along with him.

After what felt like hours, Eddie slowly rose and returned to his feet. The crowd clapped, and relief surged through me. "Don't do that again to me, okay?" I chided him after the game. "My heart can't take it!"

☙☙☙

UNMASKED

My father bounced in and out of jail that year, proving once again that he could not keep his word. A numbness formed in my heart; I no longer cared what anyone thought or what I did. I continued selling prescription drugs to kids at school, pocketing nice little wads of cash between classes. And then one day, my sneaky ways finally caught up to me.

"Mariah Nicole, please come with me," the principal said, cornering me near my locker. "We need to have a serious talk."

My heart raced as I stepped into his office and saw a police officer sitting there. "We're aware you've been selling drugs on campus," the officer said, staring me straight in the eyes. "Do you realize what a serious offense this is?"

I gulped hard. "Um, yeah, I guess?" I was only 13 years old and in the middle of the eighth grade; could they really cuff me and take me away to jail like my father?

"We'll call your parents. I'll need you to come with me," the officer said sternly.

"I can't believe you've done this!" my mother cried when she learned the news. "How could you, Mariah Nicole? Stealing my drugs and selling them to innocent kids? Really, I should send you to boot camp! Maybe that will shape you up!"

For once, I had no words. The courts sentenced me to a month in juvenile hall. I was terrified; I'd heard nightmare stories from other kids about that place. My home may have been chaotic, but I would have taken my warm bed any day over the thin covers and uncomfortable mattress that awaited me in my bare-walled room at juvenile hall.

The next 30 days were the longest of my life. I hunkered on my bed, avoiding the other kids and trying to drown out the noises down the hall and the noises in my head. No one came to visit me during that time; I had never felt more alone. *I'm not a bad kid,* I told myself. *I don't belong here with these other troublemakers.* For a few moments, my thoughts turned toward God. My grandmother said he was good, that he cared about all our troubles. My Sunday school teacher said that he loved us unconditionally. My father talked about God sometimes, too, even spouted scripture in my face. But his actions made me wonder if he and my grandmother could be talking about the same God. It was all too terribly confusing to sort out; for now, I just had to concentrate on getting out of here.

After 30 days, I was released from juvenile hall and put on probation. "You'll be getting periodic drug tests to ensure you're staying clean," my probation officer explained.

"Yes, sir," I replied, nodding swiftly. I was still smoking pot several times a day with Sam. For a moment, I considered doing what many other kids on probation did: If I got called in for a drug test, I'd simply flush my system with lots of water and test out clean. But just as quickly as I entertained the idea, I shoved it away. The lonely month I'd spent in juvenile hall had been enough

UNMASKED

for me; I was determined to clean up my ways for good.

In mid-April, my brothers and I went to stay at my Houston grandmother's home for a bit. One hot, muggy night, I slipped out back with Sam, lit up a joint and inhaled. "I'm done with this stuff," I told him. "This is going to be my last joint."

"Wow, just like that, huh?" Sam asked, lighting his own.

"Yeah. I'm done." I was only 14, but I'd been smoking pot since the age when most kids learn to ride a bike and memorize their ABCs. I'd never considered it a "real" drug, like the ones my father did, but after my scare in juvie, I didn't want to take any more chances. It was time to move on and grow up.

ঌঌঌ

That summer, my grandmother Kae Frances announced, "I'm going to send you to church camp. It's a whole week away from home, but I think you'll really enjoy it."

Though I had attended church off and on over the years, I had never been to a camp away from home with other kids my age. "What do they do all week?" I asked apprehensively.

"Oh, everything. There will be great music and games, and you'll meet some wonderful new friends, too. I think you'll love it," my grandmother replied. "You leave in a week."

SMALL TOWN TALES

I grew nervous as I packed my suitcase and prepared to leave. What if I didn't make friends? What if I didn't like it and wanted to come home?

"You'll have a great time," my mother reassured me, as she recalled her own experiences at youth camp so many years ago. "I can't wait to hear all about it."

It took me less than a day to ease into camp. The counselors were warm and welcoming, the games were fun and the worship services were even better. One night, as the stars lit up the Texas sky and the crickets came out to play, I sat on a wooden bench with dozens of my peers and listened to the speaker share about God's love.

"You may have heard all the Bible stories before, but perhaps you haven't believed they were for you. Tonight, I want you to know, God's love *is* for you. He sent his son, Jesus, to earth to die for your sins so that you could spend eternity with him in heaven. He wants to have a relationship with you, to be your best friend, someone you can talk to in times of trouble. Having a new life with Jesus doesn't mean you won't have hard times ahead, but it does mean you'll have someone by your side forever."

As I sat there, my legs curled on the bench, the soft worship music playing in the background, things finally made sense. All those times I'd thought I was alone in my pain and confusion, Jesus had been there all along. He was the missing piece in my life, the only one who could fulfill me and make me whole again. When the speaker asked who would like to accept Jesus into their heart, I slowly raised my hand. I had never wanted anything more.

UNMASKED

I prayed a prayer that night that would change my life forever. "God, I don't have all the answers, but I come to you, knowing you do. Please, forgive my sins, and be my Savior." I could hardly wait to tell my mother the good news. Being away from home had made me miss her more than ever. I vowed that when I returned I would make an effort to spend more time with her. Perhaps she, too, would want that lasting peace that could only come from Jesus.

When I got home, I told my mother all about my wonderful week at camp. "It was awesome, Mom," I gushed. "Unlike anything I've ever experienced before."

"That's great, honey." My mother's back hurt her more than ever these days; I usually found her on the couch, disoriented from her meds. Having returned from camp a new person, I saw my mother in a new light. Underneath that curly blond hair and pasted-on smile was a woman who had grown weary fighting for her family, trying to stay strong as my father broke promises and broke our hearts. Once upon a time, she had been a girl just like me, filled with dreams, hopes and desires. But along the harsh road of life, they'd been snuffed out, distant remnants beneath the high heels she donned for work every day as she tried to pay the bills. Plain and simple, life had gotten the best of her.

And it was about to get worse.

☙☙☙

SMALL TOWN TALES

We moved in with my Houston grandmother while my father looked for work. He had been out of jail for six months and once again promised us a better life. "I'm gonna find us a house to buy," he told us. "We're gonna have a good life here." He began doting on my mother again, saying all the words she wanted to hear. *I'll believe it when I see it,* I thought to myself. I was thankful I had God in my life now; he was my constant strength when all else seemed to crumble at my feet.

One afternoon, Eddie headed out to football practice, and my father took his motorcycle out for a spin. "Don't forget to wear your helmet!" my mother called after him as he revved it up in the driveway.

"I'm fine!" my father called back, disappearing around the corner without his helmet.

My mother sighed. "I wish he'd listen to me. Those things are so dangerous," she muttered.

We headed to practice to pick Eddie up. Suddenly, my mother's friend raced across the field toward us, waving her cell phone in her hand. "You need to take this!" she cried, tossing the phone to my mother. "It's important!"

I watched my mother's face go pale as she picked up the phone. "What? Okay, we'll be right down." She turned to me in shock. "Your father's been in an accident!"

The next few hours were a flurry of panic and confusion as we sped down to the local hospital to see my father. *Accident, accident* ... the word thudded in my head as the street signs blurred before us. This couldn't be happening! *Please, God, let him be okay.* With weak

UNMASKED

knees, I followed my mother into the emergency room, Eddie close behind me.

The doctors wore grim faces as we stepped into the ICU. "I'm afraid he's in bad condition," they informed us gravely. "A car going at high speed pulled out in front of him and hit him. Had he been wearing a helmet, he might only have suffered minor injuries, but the damage done to his skull is extensive."

Extensive. Slowly, I turned my head and forced myself to look at my father. Nothing could have prepared me for what I saw. Thick stitches marched across his forehead in a jagged line, strange tubes jutted out of his nose and IVs and wires covered the rest of his limp body. It was hard to believe this was the same carefree guy who had jetted off on his motorcycle a few hours before. I froze, unable to speak, move or hardly breathe.

"Is he going to make it?" my mother gasped.

"I don't think so," the doctor replied quietly. "There's been too much damage to his brain."

Not going to make it. As in, my father was going to die? Tears welled in my eyes. My father had let us down many times and made many bad choices, but nevertheless, he was still my father. He couldn't just die on us now!

"He's not going to die. He's going to be okay," my mother tried to assure me, pulling me close to her side. "We have to believe he will be okay."

As I stared at the nearly unrecognizable figure on that narrow hospital bed, my newfound faith was rattled to the core. I tried to pray, believing that God would heal my father, but instead, I only grew angry. *How could you let this happen to him?* I railed at God. *Haven't we been through enough already?*

Despite the doctor's grave words, my father fought hard to stay alive over the next several days. Slowly, he began to show small signs of improvement, surprising all the ICU staff. "It looks like he has a fighting chance," the doctor told us. "We're going to go in and remove a piece of his skull to help relieve the pressure on his brain. If that's successful, he may stand a chance at long-term recovery with the help of physical therapy."

Relief flooded us at his words. My father was not going to die! *Thank you, God,* my heart cried. *Please, heal my father.*

Pastor Kenny from my grandparents' Magnolia church, Upper Room, came to the hospital to pray over us. Though my mother was far from God, she seemed to appreciate the prayers and comfort. I thought about the speaker at camp, reminding us that God could work even difficult things in our lives for good. Could he do that right now, or would this just be another tragedy in our already hard lives?

My Houston grandmother had asked us to move out shortly before the accident, so we were now forced to live with my mother's friend. The next few weeks were a blur of hospital visits, strange new medical terms and life-changing decisions. Where would we live if my father never recovered? What would we do if he did? My mother had always been the one to hold down a steady job, but her meager income had never quite stretched far enough to pay all the bills. The promise of a new house of our own became a distant dream, replaced by more imminent things as we jumped into survival mode.

I forced myself to be strong, setting aside my pain and fear as I tried to comfort Eddie. "Everything's going to be okay," I told him. "Dad will come out of this okay. He's a fighter, remember?"

Little did I know our lives were about to change yet again.

❧❧❧

On September 5, I awoke to the sound of my mother's phone ringing. We had been trying to find my father a room with a hospital bed he could stay in long term, and I figured it must be the hospital calling. I ran into the living room, where my mother had been sleeping on the couch.

"Mom, wake up!" I hissed, nudging her gently.

When she didn't move, I grew alarmed. "Mom, wake up! Come on!" I nudged her harder this time, then shook her when she still refused to move. Panic set in as I realized that something was terribly, terribly wrong.

"Help!" I cried frantically.

My mother's friend, a nurse, raced into the room and tried to administer CPR. Eddie followed shortly and tried to wake my mother, but she was completely unresponsive. As I stood over her lifeless body crumpled on the carpet, my heart sank to a low, dark place.

SMALL TOWN TALES

I knew in my gut that my mother was gone.

Like a robot, I picked up the phone and called my grandparents. It was my grandmother's birthday and should have been a day to celebrate. Instead, I had to deliver the grim news. "Something happened to Mom." I managed to get the words out before I broke down in tears.

Our lives were catapulted into fast forward as we dealt with the unthinkable over the next few days. We learned that my mother had mixed two medications, and they'd caused her heart rate to accelerate to an unhealthy pace and then slow down to a dangerous one. Ultimately, her heart could not withstand the stimulation, and she passed away in her sleep. With my father fighting for his life in a drug-induced coma in the hospital and my mother now gone, I teetered on becoming an orphan overnight.

Where was God?

The days blurred into nights. I don't remember what I ate or what I wore or if I showered. While my peers had just begun their freshman year in high school, I was faced with greater decisions than what classes to take or which boy to like. I now had to become an adult, face the cruel world on my own.

"You can't start school until you have guardianship established," the school counselor informed me. "Have you decided where you will live?"

I stared at her, wanting to shout, "Don't you know my father's in the hospital, and my mother has just passed away?!" Instead, I replied numbly, "I'll figure it out."

UNMASKED

Pastor Kenny preached at my mother's funeral. As I sat there in my black dress, my blond hair neatly combed, a lifetime of tears threatened to come spewing out. Instead, I slipped an arm around my grieving brother and whispered, "We will be okay."

After the funeral, my grandmother approached me. "You know, before your mother died, we prayed with her, and she rededicated her heart and life to Christ."

For the first time in weeks, a glimmer of hope returned to my heart. "She did?" I cried.

"Yes. So today she is in heaven with Jesus."

Tears spilled down my cheeks at this news. "I'm so happy," I whispered.

"Have you made up your mind?" my grandmother asked. "You're running out of time."

"Eddie and I will come live with you," I told her firmly.

Two months after school started, Eddie and I finally returned to campus. I walked down the halls, listening to the chatter about the upcoming football game, homecoming dance and last week's math test. With the weight of the world on my shoulders, I felt someone had added 20 years to my life overnight. How could I giggle about boys and dances when my life hung precariously in the balance?

My father made a remarkable recovery and got out of the hospital nearly two months after his accident. Still weak and often confused, he resumed physical therapy and grieved my grandparents in his own way. "You need to live with me," he insisted to Eddie and me.

SMALL TOWN TALES

I reached far back in my memory to the times when things had been better. When I was 8, there had been a two-and-a-half-year period when my father was neither in jail nor on drugs. During that time, I'd actually seen what a functioning family looked like. He'd taken my mother on dates, showered her with gifts, attended Eddie's football games and spent time with me and Sam. We'd started to fix up our little two-bedroom house to make it feel more like a home. He'd even held down a steady job for a while. I'd tried to convince myself during that time that he had changed for good, that he could be the father I'd always wanted him to be. But eventually, he fell right back into his old ways, and the disappointment set in once again. My father would always be my father, but I had to do what I felt was best.

Eddie and I would continue to live with our grandparents, Bear and Kae Frances.

I struggled academically that year, even bringing home my first "F." I cried, for I was used to getting straight A's. There was no time for grieving, as I had to keep up my strength for Eddie and get on with our lives. We moved into the guest bedroom in my grandparents' house and slept in bunk beds. After a year, my grandparents built rooms for Eddie and me over the garage.

"Home sweet home," my grandmother said, patting the dust off her hands as we carried the last of our belongings to our new rooms. "How do you like it?"

"It's just fine. Thanks!" I smiled, grateful for all my grandparents had done. They certainly hadn't banked on

# UNMASKED

raising two teenagers this late in life. With the help of their little church, Upper Room Fellowship, they made sure all of our needs were met.

I was thankful for a roof over our heads and a bed to sleep in, but the stubborn ache in my stomach remained. I had yet to deal with my pain.

☙☙☙

It didn't take my father long after his recovery to land himself back in jail. His actions confirmed my decision to live with my grandparents. Eddie threw himself back into football, while I tried to keep up in school. My migraines persisted, sometimes growing so painful that I could not move.

"Jesus, we ask you to heal Mariah Nicole of her headaches, in the authority given to us in the name of Jesus," my grandmother prayed.

To my amazement, the migraines subsided, and we both praised the Lord for my healing. I had developed an on-again/off-again relationship with the Lord, sometimes crying out to him and other times feeling nothing but anger toward him. My grandparents had begun taking us to the Upper Room church every Sunday. The pastor, PK, reached out to us with such genuine warmth. And the people were kind and friendly. I wanted the deep relationship with Christ they possessed, but I didn't know how to move forward from my pain and anger.

On my 17th birthday, I learned that my Florida

grandfather, whom I'd grown close with over the years, had passed away after a long battle with diabetes. The pent-up tears I'd been holding back for years suddenly came like a flood, and I fell to the floor in hysterics at the news of his death. The hurt from my father's reckless lifestyle, the accident, my mother's death and the many changes I'd endured at such a young age came rushing at me all at once. I was a broken girl.

My grandfather Bear walked into my room to console me. "I'm so sorry, honey," he whispered, rubbing my back as the tears flowed. "You cry all you like now. Get it all out."

I knew I had lashed out at my grandparents many times unfairly since moving in with them, yet they had remained patient and loving all the way. Their unconditional love meant everything to me at a time when my world was crumbling at my feet. Just like Jesus, they had always been a constant source of strength and guidance in my life, even when I had not wanted it or known I'd needed it.

They say that after a long rain the most beautiful flowers bloom. My life had been more than a long rain; it had been one raging storm after another. Yet after that night, something changed inside of me, and the teeniest bud of a flower poked its way out of the ground. My heart slowly softened, and I turned over my grief to the capable, loving hands of my heavenly father. I immersed myself in my grandparents' church, proud to now call it my own. The folks at Upper Room became like second family to

UNMASKED

Eddie and me, praying over us and loving on us every Sunday.

❧❧❧

"How can I pray for you today?" a kind woman asked after the service one week.

"Pray that my father finally turns from his ways and accepts Christ," I replied. "Thank you so much."

I returned to reading my Bible and found great comfort in the words. Since I was a young girl, I had always known about God's love and his truths, but now, they truly came alive to me. I realized that the sustaining presence in my life had always been the Lord. He was the one who had carried me through the darkness when my father failed to come home at night. He was the one who had held my hand when I'd seen my mother pass away before my eyes. And he was the one who would walk before me in whatever new trials came my way. I was never alone.

My grandmother Kae Frances took me to the women's retreat with our church every year, held at Texas Bible Institute in Columbus, a little more than an hour from Magnolia. As I walked the beautiful campus and began to pray, I felt God prompting my heart. "This is the college I want you to go to," he said.

Could I have heard him right? How would I ever afford to go to Bible college? I had recently landed a job at a retail store, but tuition for Bible college was probably thousands of dollars. Was this a bit of a stretch, or would God provide a way?

I confided in my grandmother about Bible college.

"God will make a way if it's meant to be," she encouraged me.

Eddie, two years behind me, is extremely smart and talks about going to school to become a youth pastor. I prayed and felt God leading me in the direction of working with children, perhaps working alongside a youth pastor. I knew there were many children like myself, many with their own tragic tales, many who had kept their wounds and scars to themselves as they lived in their own world of hurt. Perhaps I could share my story of Jesus' healing in my life with them.

As I read my Bible one night, my eyes fell onto a favorite passage, John 3:17: "For God did not send his son into the world to condemn the world, but to save the world through him." I thought of my father, back in jail again, still nursing his wounds with the cares of the world. I no longer felt angry but instead looked at him as a broken man in need of a Savior. While I had long ago stopped believing in my father's empty promises, I had never stopped believing that God could change his heart for good.

❧❧❧

"Hey, Sis! How's it going?"

It was Sam on the other line. Sam and I still kept in

UNMASKED

touch often; he planned to move to be closer to us before I left for college. "Doing good. Just counting down the days till I leave. I'm getting so excited! How are you?"

"Same," Sam replied coolly. Sam was still on his own path, not quite ready to give his heart over to Christ. He was another one I was praying for, and I knew that my requests were in good hands.

We chatted for a few more minutes as I packed my things. God had indeed made a way for me to attend Texas Bible Institute. After I hung up, I wandered over to the window of my bedroom and peered out for a moment. Fall would be here soon, and the trees would burst into color, turning our little town of Magnolia into a picturesque paradise. Some folks would stop to admire the postcard-worthy view, while others would quickly pass on by as they headed out of town, leaving a trail of dust behind. And this time, I would follow them, saying goodbye to one chapter of my life as I embarked on another.

But I'll be back with more stories to tell. I am certain of that.

CLOSING THE BOOK
The Story of Kendra
Written by Marty Minchin

With the wide Montana sky stretching out behind her, my friend Leigh explained why she couldn't hang out that afternoon.

"My mom caught me. I'm in big trouble, and I'm grounded." She pushed her long mousy-brown hair behind her shoulder.

My stomach sank with disappointment. We had just moved to this sprawling mountainside neighborhood from Texas, and Leigh was my only friend so far. She was bossy and overbearing, but she was better than nothing.

"What happened?" I asked, wondering what could be so bad that her parents would ground her. We spent most of our summer days tooling around on bicycles or riding Arabian horses with Leigh's mom, and there wasn't a lot of time left over to get in that much trouble.

"I was on my mom's computer looking at something, and she found out what it was," Leigh replied.

"What did you look up?"

"I Googled 'naked men.'"

What's the big deal? I thought. My religious, conservative dad and my older brother wouldn't even walk around the house without a shirt on, and I certainly had never seen a man naked.

Leigh slunk off toward her house across the street, and

UNMASKED

I headed straight to my parents' computer. My curiosity was piqued.

N-A-K-E-D M-E-N, I typed into the search engine.

Pictures and articles galore popped up on the screen, opening up a world as vast as the landscape outside. The images didn't really interest me, but the stories did. My parents checked out piles of books for me, but I finished them so quickly that I was bored before the next trip to the library. Here was an endless supply of intriguing new reading material.

I was a few months shy of 9 years old.

❧❧❧

When I was growing up, my father favored me over my half-brother, Zach, who wasn't his child. My mom had married Dad three months after divorcing an abusive man she had been married to for seven years. She was insecure, and my dad made her feel safe.

He was tall, a former pipeline welder whose once muscular body softened into a beer belly by the time I was a toddler. He had a big hawk nose and a bigger smile, which everyone loved about him. He laughed a lot, and on the outside, people believed he was a great husband and father.

But in our doublewide trailer outside Dallas, our family life didn't quite reflect Dad's sterling reputation.

He disdained my mom, and as I grew into his personal confidante, he shared with me details of their marriage as

CLOSING THE BOOK

if I was his best friend, not his daughter. He yelled at her, and if she did something he didn't like, he would ignore her until she apologized and said it was her fault. Meanwhile, he was showing me that there was no value in the covenant between a man and a woman.

When I was about 6 years old, I watched through the living room window as my mom and dad fought in our wooded backyard. The ground was covered with leaves, and the trees towered over them as they screamed back and forth, my dad jabbing my mom with his finger.

I picked up the phone and called my cousin.

"My parents are fighting, and I don't know what to do," I said, my voice shaking as I stared out the window.

"That means they're going to get a divorce," she said.

"What's that?"

"That means your parents don't live together or talk to each other anymore."

A hollow despair gripped me in the belly. *Surely that could never happen to my parents.*

But I wasn't so sure.

❧❧❧

My dad's brother was a preacher, and we were always involved in church. Jesus was a frequent topic of conversation at our house. One night, I felt certain I wanted Jesus to become a very personal part of my life. My parents were deeply religious, and Mom knelt beside me while Dad stood next to us.

UNMASKED

"Do you know what that means?" Mom asked gently.

"It means I want Jesus to be in my heart and be with me forever."

The sweet sounds of my dad's special prayer language hovered over us as I repeated the prayer to ask Jesus to be my Savior. I told Jesus that I was sorry for all of the wrong things I had done, and I knew that he was forgiving me for all of them. Dad set his huge hands on my shoulders, and a warmth radiated through my back. My mom couldn't stop smiling.

"How does it feel?" Mom asked as she wiped the tears from her cheeks.

"I feel full, but I'm tired." I left our intimate little circle and headed back to bed.

Soon after, my Uncle Jim baptized me in two feet of water in an above-ground pool in our backyard. As he dunked me, cheers rose from the 40 friends and family who had come to celebrate with a barbecue.

❧❧❧

I saw so much hypocrisy at home and with my parents' church leader friends growing up that if I hadn't seen angels when I was 7 years old, I'd probably be an atheist now.

When someone in our family got sick, my parents believed in praying before seeing a doctor. That's why after three days of running a very high fever, I was still at home.

CLOSING THE BOOK

My dad sat next to me on the bed, washing my eyes and forehead with a cool cloth.

"What are you looking at?" he asked, watching as my eyes tracked something he couldn't see behind him.

"I'm watching the angel up there. He's flying over your head and going in circles. He's small."

"Really?"

"Now he's flying over there." I pointed to the corner of the room. "Now over there."

The idea of seeing angels was not a foreign one. My parents had told me stories about my uncle seeing angels, and I thought it happened to everyone.

During those three days, which mesh into one day in my memory, I saw more than 150 angels. They were all sizes, from thumbnail to one that was longer than our doublewide trailer. I saw male and female, winged and wingless angels. They looked like the angels in the poster on my wall of a guardian angel helping two children across a bridge.

Eventually, the angels faded away, all except one life-sized female angel who stood in the doorway of my closet and looked at me.

I found my mom in the living room to tell her.

"There's an angel standing in my closet."

My mom was unfazed. "Go ask her what her name is."

I did.

"Angela," she replied. I closed my eyes for a moment, and she was gone when I opened them.

"Where are you?"

UNMASKED

"I'm right beside you in bed." Her voice was a murmur in my ear. "It's time for you to go to sleep."

When I woke up, my fever was gone. My parents suspect I may have had a form of meningitis, but I never saw a doctor about it.

※※※

I didn't see my mom much during those years, as she had started a consulting business. My mom and dad had prayed for an idea that would allow them to work from home and move around because they didn't want to stay in Texas.

My mom is extremely intelligent, and she made the business a success at a time when most similar businesses were failing. She sometimes worked as many as 16 hours a day, in part because my dad wouldn't help her.

His reason? He said his job was to be the prayer warrior for the business.

Mom made a lot of money, one time earning a quarter of a million dollars in a year. After a short stint in Redmond, Washington, my parents decided to move to Montana. They traded in our doublewide for a 4,000-square-foot house on 10 acres with our own pond.

That summer, while Leigh was grounded, I developed a porn addiction.

At age 8, I didn't know anything about sex or anatomy. My theory was that when people got married, God somehow made a woman pregnant.

CLOSING THE BOOK

The day my computer screen filled with pictures and words about sex, I had no idea what was going on. I loved to read and learn, and here was a ton of new information.

I gravitated more toward the erotic stories, which were available for free online. They were similar to Harlequin romances, but leaving no detail untold. I couldn't get enough.

I was sneaky, and the Internet was easy to access. I read stories on my phone, on my laptop, on my dad's computer. Sometimes I'd copy a long story into a Word document, print it out and slide it between the mattresses on my bed. Then I'd erase all traces of my searches for stories on the computer.

I'd read late into the night, and if my parents asked what I was doing, I'd tell them I was reading for my online homeschooling courses or instant messaging with a friend. One of my chores was taking out the trash, and I'd slip my hard copies into the garbage on the way out the door. Soon I was reading as much as eight hours a day.

In a decade of porn addiction, I was only caught once, when I was 14. I slouched in front of the computer one afternoon, the screen white on the left with text and blue on the right with graphics. Dad was on one of his walks, and he knocked on the window and waved when he saw me inside.

Startled, I clicked the browser closed and smiled at Dad, barely hiding my guilty expression. When he came in to check on me moments later, I had clicked onto a benign Web site.

UNMASKED

"What were you looking at?" he asked.

"Nothing." I kept my voice nonchalant, but he wasn't buying it.

"Then show it to me."

As devious as I could be, I couldn't think of any Web site that even resembled the blue and white screen the story was on. I reluctantly pulled up the erotic tale.

Dad's eyes widened as he read over my shoulder. "What is this?" he asked, but he didn't wait for an answer. "You need to come upstairs for a talk."

I knew I was in trouble.

Mom sat silently in the living room while Dad lectured me on the inappropriateness of what I was reading and expressed his great disappointment in what I was doing. He handed me a Bible and sent me to my room to read the book in it called "Song of Solomon" and not to come out until I figured out what I needed to learn from it.

"You'll know when to come back," he said.

I read the story of Solomon and his wife's great love for each other, and I quickly understood what Dad wanted.

"Love is supposed to be sacred," I told him, forcing out a few tears. "Love is supposed to be between one man and one woman."

That was it. My only punishment. I went right back to the stories, often reading late after midnight when my parents were asleep. I never once felt guilty for deceiving my parents or for what I was reading.

CLOSING THE BOOK

❧❧❧

I read porn well into my teenage years. At the height of it, I'd wake up at 6 a.m. and read for 30 minutes, then get ready and go to school. I'd read for an hour or two after school, do my homework and spend time with my boyfriend. At about 9:30 p.m., I'd say goodnight to my parents and then read until 2 or 3 a.m.

The alarm would go off again at 6 a.m. On the weekends, I might stay up reading until 5 or 6 a.m. Needless to say, I wasn't getting enough sleep.

No one found out about my addiction, and as I got older, I'd tell myself I'd just read until I got married. Maybe I did it because I was alone all the time with a brother that was much older. My parents were always fighting, and I had an abundance of free time on my hands. Somehow, despite my strict religious upbringing and my own relationship with God, it just slipped by my morals.

❧❧❧

Several years went by. We moved to Magnolia. I still hadn't told anybody about my reading habits. I had started dated someone seriously. Drake and I shared the same faith, and I didn't dare tell him about my nightly reading habits. I knew that if he found out, it would hurt him terribly. I sometimes tried to stop, but that never lasted more than two weeks or a month. My reading had expanded into stories about more experimental sexual

UNMASKED

practices, and I couldn't stay away. My mind constantly wandered to the Web sites and to the ones I could be reading right then, especially if I was bored at night and couldn't go to sleep.

Dating Drake forced me to rearrange my schedule so that I could feed my addiction without him finding out. The tradeoff was sleep for reading, which meant I'd often take naps at lunchtime to make up for the night before.

My whole life felt out of whack, and I sank into almost a depressed state sometimes. When I walked down the halls of my high school, my fellow students acted like the character stereotypes I'd learned from the pornographic stories. The girls seemed ditzy, and the guys only had one thing on their minds. It became difficult to separate the real people from the characters, and in the end, I just decided that all adults, including these teenagers, could not be trusted. I grew suspicious of all people's motives, whether they were giving me a hug or telling me something about God.

That included Drake. Could I trust that this guy wasn't using me? For several months, I wouldn't even hold his hand in public. In my mind, though, I cast us as characters in one of the stories, and I struggled with lust. It was hard to be alone with him.

The disconnection between my inner and outer lives grew even more apparent when I talked to kids who thought I had it "all together" and looked up to me in high school.

Some of them would tell me they were struggling with

CLOSING THE BOOK

pornography, and I knew all of the right things to say.

"You need to give it up," I'd tell them. Did I listen to my own advice? No. For some reason, I didn't think that was a big deal, and I felt no guilt about it.

At a church camp that July, the pastor talked about a topic that hit home.

"A porn addiction can destroy not only you, but the people you love."

I rarely make emotional displays, but tears were already forming.

"Porn's allure can be so strong that only God can free you from its grasp. If a porn addiction has a hold on you, let God's power fight it. Let God give you the strength to resist."

The words were hitting me so hard I could hardly breathe.

I was surrounded by a crowd of high school kids, friends. I wept so hard that I couldn't hold my head up.

God! I don't know what to do. I don't know how to handle this, and I can't get rid of this on my own. I don't think I can hide my addiction much longer, and I'm going to be exposed if I don't take this step. I know it grieves your heart when I do this, and I don't want to hurt you or others.

For the first time in my life, I felt a big twinge of conviction that what I was reading was wrong.

It was time to change.

ঌঌঌ

UNMASKED

A week or two later, I told my boyfriend, Drake, I needed to talk to him. We were seriously considering marriage. I confessed everything.

If I had continued running around behind his back trying to read more, it would be an adulterous relationship — with pornography. Instead of focusing on Drake if we should get married, my thoughts would have turned to stories of other people having sex. I feared that our marriage would become superficial, or even worse, end in divorce. God's healing freed me to concentrate my mind on Drake and our relationship.

Drake's forgiveness flowed easily; he told me he wasn't perfect, either.

Now that I had ditched my "undercover reading habits" and was getting more sleep, I could meet Drake for lunch, where we read the Bible together and discussed what we were learning. It created a strength in our relationship that we didn't have before and continues to bond us spiritually. We've become each other's accountability partners, no longer hiding our secrets.

☙☙☙

My mom left my dad in the fall of 2009. I stayed with my dad, still deceived by a lifetime of his lies about my mother's incompetence. In fact, I thought my mother was foolish for moving out. My contempt for her grew so great that I wouldn't even talk to her on the phone.

By Christmas, my dad was treating me like he had

CLOSING THE BOOK

treated my mom, rather than as his trusted friend, his only daughter. He ignored me when he was angry, waiting for me to admit my wrongdoing and apologize. Worst of all, he turned on Drake, who he had concluded was no longer perfect for me. Drake couldn't provide for me, Dad would say. He wasn't ambitious enough to further himself in life. Dad's comments stabbed into my heart, and slowly the scales fell from my eyes.

Finally, after 18 years, I understood what my dad was about.

I had been reconnecting with my mom, spending a weekend with her here and there and talking some on the phone.

I poured out to her my distress over how Dad talked about Drake, about how if I said anything against his opinions he'd bulldoze right through it and keep me up for hours, wearing me down until I agreed with him.

"What am I supposed to do, Mom? I'm not leaving Drake, but he's my dad."

"Actually, you can tell him to stop," she said. "You're an adult, and you have a say in what people around you say. If something makes you upset, you can tell him, 'I don't like it when you say that.'"

I went back to Dad's and tried that, but things just got worse.

"Why do you even want to live with him?" Mom asked the next weekend after I recounted the disastrous week.

"I don't know," I blurted out. "Why am I living with him?"

UNMASKED

Too frightened to confront him in person, I called Dad with the news.

"I'm not coming home. I'm moving in with Mom, and nothing you say will change my mind."

First, silence.

"I'm very disappointed," Dad finally said. "I can't believe you would do this to your only family."

He doesn't think that my mom and brother are his family anymore. He has done this all to himself.

That was the last straw, and my mom, brother and a family friend moved my things from Dad's to Mom's. I didn't see my dad for two months, but after experimenting with meeting him for dinner every Tuesday night, I realized that the stress he caused me was affecting all of my other relationships. Dad was still stuck in the past, and I couldn't do that with him anymore.

❧❧❧

Unlike my dad, my new friends at Upper Room were transparent, showing me what a genuine Christian lives like — one who doesn't say one thing and do another.

Many people at our church smoke. One in particular struggled for years, unable to put the cigarettes down. Instead of trying to hide it, he was open about his struggle, asking our church to pray for him and talk to him about whether he was still smoking. He wasn't trying to be perfect. Instead, he invited us to help him through a hard time.

CLOSING THE BOOK

Another church friend worried that his children were suffering because of his fascination with ghosts and horror movies. The children woke up screaming from nightmares and frequently were frightened. I could tell he didn't really want to give up his guilty pleasure, but he was willing to for the sake of his children. Over a month or so, I saw him separate himself from his supernatural interests.

As I watched people admit their faults, my prayers changed. I had always praised God, thanked him and asked him for help. I felt free to confess that I, too, was not perfect.

My heart was opened for complete transformation.

☙☙☙

Letting go of my addiction has opened up a new world to me, a world I've always wanted. Because my family moved every few years, I never made close friends. In fact, I've never had even one best friend until now.

I'm not tired in the mornings anymore, so I can meet my new best friend at the gym to work out. The energy I used to spend scheming to hide my addiction I now pour into planning events for our church.

Drake and I recently spent the evening with two couples from Upper Room. The three girls are best friends, as are the three guys.

One couple is newly married, and Drake and I and the other couple are dating. We're all young, all earnestly seeking God.

UNMASKED

All around the living room, friends lounged on the couch, draped casually on the furniture in this one-bedroom apartment. We discussed God and theology, with someone occasionally breaking out in prayer. God's presence filled this intimate gathering, and I basked in the closeness of it.

Finally, I have friends — best friends — who are like-minded. My relationship with Drake is stronger than ever.

I've closed the books of porn that consumed years of my life, and now I have turned to another book — the Bible — with great friends to help me on my journey.

CORE VALUE
The Story of Eric
Written by Richard Drebert

Shock had thrown open the hood, and someone seemed to be *tinkering*. Depression broke off bolts and wrenched in places that shouldn't be touched in a man's mind, and I screamed an end to it. Booze didn't numb me to the cold iron anymore.

I had buried my brother Phil in a wrecking yard of joyless years. Cancer killed my father. Mental illness plagued my mother — and depression had swamped both my brothers like a Texas flood. Our brand of religion seemed to fuel my family's depression, rage and self-pity and, in the end, could not save any of us.

I had a plot reserved in that same wrecking yard with Phil — but how soon? I thought.

For me, it had all started with Dad.

ৡৡৡ

I was the youngest of three sons, and a decade separated my middle brother and me. My oldest brother was 11 years ahead of me, and when I was 2, we all lived in a one-room shanty near a tiny Texas town, about 10 miles west of Lake Livingston.

Our town of Livingston had about 5,000 folks scattered on the Polk County Seat. We lived a few miles

UNMASKED

out of town as the crow flies, four miles off the pavement at the end of a long, windy dirt road. Over the years Dad nailed more and more rooms to the house, until Mom had a 40-by-40-foot home — but it still wasn't big enough for us to be happy.

My dad had dated and then married my mama, a blue-eyed blond Cajun girl from Houma, Louisiana (about an hour from New Orleans), where Dad turned wrenches as a mechanic for a spell. He took Mama to Houston, then bought a little patch of Texas woods in Livingston from my grandpa.

My father's ways were as different as oil and water from Grandpa's, who was raised in Mississippi. Grandpa was a hardscrabble cooper (wood barrel maker) and blacksmith and could build about anything, except a proper family. He married and outlived three wives, and the way we best kept track of some of his offspring was by labeling them with the maiden names of his wives.

Dad eschewed my grandpa's lifestyle. He became a strict Baptist man, who never left my mama, despite their bitter squabbles. When he promised "till death do us part," Mama could count on it — no dilly-dalliance or divorce. The nuts and bolts of his religion gave him a schematic to follow in his life, but no enjoyment. His true satisfaction only came from his work as a master mechanic.

My dad launched Livingston Garage, the best place in Polk County to get your points, rotor and distributor cap replaced, with a set of new Champion sparkplugs gapped

CORE VALUE

just right. Locals got an honest estimate on auto and truck repair, and soon Dad added a parts house to his wrench-turning enterprise.

"Good afternoon, Livingston Garage."

As secretary, Mama manned the phones and kept the books (and *me* from playing under truck tires), and the business flourished in some years and floundered in others, as family endeavors will. I toddled after Mama, the grease monkey's baby, bare feet tracking oily toe-prints on the carpets.

Mama took comfort from her boy — comfort that Dad could have given, had he a mind to. Mama's psyche was troubled and growing vulnerable as the years passed, and I seemed to be her only solace.

When I was only 2, my mama's mental stability started to deteriorate, and she began to talk about crucifying me because the prophesy needed to be fulfilled. My dad stayed with Mama to protect us boys, because back then we would have been alone with her if they were to divorce.

After Mama went into the mental facilities a couple of times and seemed to be on the uphill crawl back to reality, my oldest brother, Mason, took over where she left off. He attempted suicide by overdosing when he was 18, only to fry his brain. I was 8 at the time. (Mason is now in his 50s but acts like he's 5. I haven't seen him in years.)

Around that time, my routines included elementary school, church and an occasional fishing trip with my dad at Lake Livingston in our flat bottom boat. I talked to

UNMASKED

myself a lot in the summertime — no one else was around at home. Pedaling under the broiling Texas sun to my nearest friend three miles away didn't thrill me, and I kept my own company, hunting and fishing as I grew out of adolescence.

ಎಂಎಂಎಂ

In the woods, I shot 'em dead: foxes and cats.

We boys called the big Texas red squirrels "foxes" and the skittish gray squirrels (more stealthy and harder to hunt) "cats." Mama fried them or stewed them up, and every redneck in the county would have given their eyeteeth for a taste.

Church sermons were getting harder to swallow when I was 15. Our family went to the Baptist church because my grandpa did before he died.

Deep Southern tradition demanded that I fill a pew on Sundays and Wednesday nights without excuse, unless I was coughing up a lung. My brothers had moved away from home, but I still resented them — especially Phil, Dad's pride and joy. If I learned to drive a stick shift, he told me that Phil had *never* ground a gear when he drove. If I ran the 40-yard dash at school, Phil had run it faster when he was my age. He played football better (a legend in Livingston football, still to this day!). No matter what I did, my father held up my brother as an icon that I could never touch. On the other hand, my mama favored Mason. He was funnier than I was. Mason cooked better

CORE VALUE

than me. Mason needed more attention with school. I was always lost in the middle in my family. The youngest, the forgotten.

I carried a permanent putdown in my heart that I finally blamed on Dad's religion. God always expected more than I could pump out, and I felt that people at church looked at me as inferior somehow. I grew to hate those squeaky hardwood pews, and I prayed to heaven for the day when I was old enough to fly the coop.

When I was 16, I hot-rodded across Livingston in my Chevrolet pickup truck and told Dad I was attending the bigger Baptist church there — but his snoops dropped by the garage for a tune-up, and my snow job melted fast. At my new church, I never walked past the foyer. I shook hands just long enough to receive my church bulletin and skedaddled to my waiting buds.

Some old deacon must have ratted me out to Dad, and I was pouting like a pup beside him at Grandpa's old church again, quick as a heartbeat.

My '77 long-bed Chevy, with a 350-cubic-inch engine, drove me wild with freedom, and my lone-wolf days ended. I made friends in high school, and the taste of independence got sweeter as I ran with guys who smoked dope and drank. Marijuana depressed me, dragging my mind into pits of despair, and I hated the feeling, yet the dreamy drug haze seduced me back time and again.

Mom and Dad suspected that I was "using," but were too busy running the garage and trying to keep their marriage off the rocks to watch me like a hawk.

UNMASKED

"I seen a new 'Do Not Enter' sign up on the highway, man."

"We'll grab it tonight! Two o'clock sound right?"

I valued my mechanic's tools like a surgeon's instruments, and I could nab a street sign like nobody's business. My cohorts and I hid our stash of signs in the woods outside of town, and we siphoned off a few to post in our bedrooms — to remind us of our bodacious coups.

By 17, my teenage shenanigans were getting old. Changing car oil and sweeping up greasy cat litter kept me busy after school most days and in the summers; Dad educated me in his trade from the floor *up* — a career that might not make a man rich in Texas, but was a necessary evil for most, like a lawyer or doctor.

Sometimes I hated the sight of the garage's old cinderblock building, where I degreased every boring socket and screwdriver. But I did enjoy a couple major distractions: Graduation loomed on my horizon, and a particular junior with chestnut hair and hazel eyes had stolen my heart the first day I saw her in a business class. She labored on a manual typewriter, one that dinged like a bell, over and over, after every line she typed.

I studied Lisa's beautiful face for a few days and finally settled on the best way to dazzle her: "Y'all gonna let that thing call you a ding-a-ling, like that?"

She was 16 when her friend talked her into dating me. After our second outing, I let her know that I was planning to marry her, and it kindled tender, heartfelt words I shall always treasure.

CORE VALUE

"Eric, you're full of it! You don't even know me. How can you love me and want to marry me?"

Lisa had come from the same iron-fisted religious background as me. We both knew Jesus and held tight to our get-out-of-hell pass, but this "God" that our parents served stood far out of our reach when we were in a pickle. And growing up with the older church folk in the community confirmed to us that they attended services for social reasons, rather than to talk to anyone in heaven. And God certainly never talked back.

Phil sent occasional letters from deployments with the Army, while my other brother, Mason, barely stayed afloat in his own sea of emotional crises — like my mom. Her mind grew more fragile, and worries troubled her, while her marriage to Dad stretched thinner with every passing year.

❧❧❧

"Do you take this man …?"

Lisa said "I do," but I could hardly be called a man. I was just 18, and Lisa was barely 18. We stood in her living room together, surrounded by family and well wishers, quietly pledging to treat our union differently than our own parents had — without a clue *how* to do it.

"I'll bet you $200 your marriage doesn't last two years," Phil wagered.

I took the bet, wondering if he knew something I didn't.

UNMASKED

We ended the ceremony and drove straight to Lisa's senior prom to cap off a long night.

Arguments started within the first few months of our wedded bliss. My only example of how to be a husband had been my father. My mother was Dad's second wife — his first had run off with his best friend, and his story had burrowed deep in my consciousness. An ominous mistrust of women had rooted in my mind, tainting our marriage relationship from the beginning.

Headstrong Lisa balked at my bullying, and she landed a job at a publishing company, while I donned coveralls at Dad's garage each day. I completed training at Universal Technical Institute in automotive and truck technologies, and we hoped to work our way into bright financial daylight.

Lisa and I attended church sporadically, hungering for something other than potlucks and altar calls, and at home we tried to find areas in our lives that we had in common — like a baby. No baby came like everyone was expecting, and we began to worry why.

We were married about three years when cancer sabotaged my mom and dad. I watched my strong, robust father, with arms like a wrestler and hard as nails, crumble in pain and shed his health in a matter of months. Just when he had become my best friend, Dad passed away, out of control and weak as a child — not at all the way he lived and worked.

He carried his faith with him to his grave, scuffed and chipped, but still intact. After Dad died, Mason attempted

CORE VALUE

suicide again and went into another mental hospital. He has been a ward of the State of Texas since his first suicide attempt.

After Dad's death, I searched for solid handholds to latch onto, and I seized upon a hereditary selfishness as my heirloom — the legacy from my grandfather and the wrecking ball for at least two generations of our family.

Mom needed special care, and it immediately fell to Lisa and me. Our automotive business languished when Texas built a bypass that stole traffic from Livingston, and I ran the garage for a few money-draining years. When a buyer put up funds enough to get Mom out of debt, I jumped at the chance, and we sold the whole kit and caboodle.

❧❧❧

Our daughter — our miracle.

I held Kristin with calloused hands, scared witless, praying and wondering how I could possibly raise a girl. Money was tight. For eight tempestuous years, we had been trying to have a child, but it wasn't until we surrounded ourselves with people who believed the Bible that our hearts reached out to God.

"We'll agree with you and Lisa, that God gives you a baby ..."

These wonderful Assemblies of God friends prayed with us, and their care opened a door to God's love. Our emotions ran high at first, like the nearby Trinity River at flood stage. Then Lisa just kicked back and let God do what he wanted and *relaxed*.

I never voiced the weird feelings I was dealing with at the time: I didn't know if I would be a good father. Look at my family! How much of my life did I have to revamp if I had a child? I'd never been around kids much, and "baby" was a word that sent my knees to knockin'. In the hospital room, those little frail pink toes and fingers sent me into a panic. My whole life was changing — I had no idea how much.

Every respiratory allergy in Texas seemed to trouble our baby girl. We walked and rocked Kristin in two-hour shifts, medicating her and pacing through bouts of colic, until our nerves wore down to nubbins. Sometimes Lisa's dad or mom would drive to Livingston to relieve us — and sleep never felt sooo good!

☙☙☙

Broke.
Doctors and nurses. Tests and blood work. Tubes and paperwork. The first year of Kristin's life seemed like I overhauled an engine without an instruction manual. It seemed like almost every cent of my paychecks went to pay hospital bills, and we decided to move closer to Houston doctors. We chose Magnolia as our base of operations and found a doublewide trailer not far from my work as a mechanic. My Automotive Service Excellence and Master Automotive certifications helped me land a

CORE VALUE

good job, and we joined a church that seemed to fit our needs.

But self-centeredness still jam-packed my mind whenever I thought about where we *could* have been — if we had just had a child who was not sick all the time. I wouldn't be in debt. We probably wouldn't be stressed out all the time. Sometimes, I wrongfully blamed Lisa and Kristin and thought it was their fault we were in this predicament.

"Your daughter may have leukemia." It seemed to be a last straw, and we worried through a battery of tests, but no sign of the disease showed up. Praise God!

Somebody's messin' with our heads.

At times when I prayed, I heard God plainly, warning me about my pride and unkindness toward Lisa, but a choir of other voices in my head accused everyone *else* for my problems. As through a heavy mist, I sometimes perceived a battle line of evil arrayed against me — then just as suddenly, the mist obscured it, and I was blind again to anything "spiritual."

Christmas turned out to be the best family get-together we had ever experienced. My brother Phil was home from his stint in the Army and worked as a supervisor at a railroad car fabrication plant. He picked up Mom and brought her to his house, and we feasted and chatted about old times. So much water over the dam, but the future seemed a little brighter that day for my family. After years of resentment, Phil was now one of my best friends.

UNMASKED

At the first of the new year, Phil called me.

"Looks like I'll be taking some time off, Eric. I quit the plant and need some time to regroup."

Phil had been embroiled in three divorces, and I knew he struggled with depression sometimes, too. I was happy to see him take a vacation.

"I'll be gone for a couple weeks or more, so don't worry."

I didn't worry — until three weeks had passed and calls to his cell phone went straight to his voice mail. Then his phone just rang and rang, like it hung somewhere in the ether …

"Lisa, we're going to see what's up."

Phil owned a nice house in Liberty and lived alone. He was an inventor at heart; creative, but inept, like my grandfather, when it came to keeping a family together. I pulled into the wide driveway and surveyed his immaculate tan and red brick home, and I thought about Dad, so very proud of Phil's accomplishments. Gulf coast hurricanes, Texas twisters and wildfires can't compare to the devastation we were about to witness.

While Lisa and Kristin waited in the front yard, I pushed open his unlocked door and stood in the dimly lit hallway where a sickening smell of death draped me from head to toe. I thought I would puke. It took all my courage to step into the next room, where my brother was laying on the living room floor covered in blood. The coroner estimated that he had taken his life 45 days earlier. I tried to be strong on my own.

CORE VALUE

Two hours after finding his decomposed body, in a conference room in her nursing home, I shakily told Mama that Phil was gone. I had to call my nephews and tell them their dad was dead by his own doing. I had to prepare the funeral arrangements.

It took time for us to piece together Phil's traumas: divorce issues, separating himself from his kids, heavy medications for mental illness — and seemingly no relief in sight.

While I numbly tried to find a handle on my grief, the whole family saga pinned me like a fallen oak: Mental illness might claim me, too.

When is it my turn? Would my own suicide be written in the family history?

God, where are you in all of this? How could you let this happen to my family?

Lisa's parents, her sister, Tanya, brother-in-law, Shawn, and some special Christian friends from our church refused to watch tragedy steal hope from Lisa, Kristin and me. We were drowning in insurance forms, tax documents and property issues — and they dove into our bedlam to help us settle Phil's estate. They showed faith and love when it was not easy to help.

The day I opened the door to Phil's house, Lisa, Tanya and Shawn braced against the heavy smell of decomposing flesh bonded to woodwork, papers and furniture. Lisa and I truly experienced "Jesus" for the first time through our brother and sister.

He sat with us at the desk sifting through documents,

UNMASKED

Jesus helped us clean the house and later, Jesus stuck by us through the funeral itself.

And I was a jerk through it all.

I felt my rage at God gaining RPMs, and I turned to drinking for comfort. I worked long hours at an auto shop and kept up a brave front at church, but Lisa worried. She never knew if she might arrive home from her job at a local hospital and find me sacked out in my easy chair — or worse, like my brother Phil. Kristin wouldn't sleep in her own room, worried that her daddy would try to kill himself because Grannie, Uncle Phil and Uncle Mason all attempted this at some point in their lives.

Self-pity blanketed me, and my family could barely stand to be near me.

For months after my brother's death, I struggled to keep my head on straight. I managed to uphold the family tradition of church attendance with Lisa and Kristin, but my heart strayed far from my immediate family. I was as close as a man could be to "shipwrecked faith," and if I wasn't bipolar, I certainly was MOODY.

One night, Lisa shouted, "What has happened to you by your family sucks, but you have to snap out of it, because I refuse to allow you to leave that legacy to your daughter!"

That was a major turning point for me.

Everyone, including my girls, Lisa and Kristin, could have thrown me overboard, but instead, he or she loved me closer and closer to an unalterable truth hard for me to accept: *God loved me right where I struggled.* Even while anger tainted my faith, God didn't scold me. He gently touched my heart, reminding me that he waited for my decision to give up my life to him, once and for all.

❧❧❧

Direction. Vision. Purpose.

These had drifted in a haze of marijuana smoke, unreal to me as far back as my teens. To get my mind around the idea that Jesus, the Creator of heaven and earth, was my "friend" was as foreign to me as altering my family DNA — impossible. I knew that God was real, and Jesus had bled on the cross to give me a pass to heaven, but to know this person was beyond my grasp.

So Jesus reached out to *me*.

I had *seen* him in my family and friends, and in the following years, the fetid mist that blinded me to my own self-centered ways began to roll back. It was a terrorizing moment when I suddenly stood alone against generations of lust, greed, rage, unforgiveness. They lived in my DNA, and like an army, they marched against my mind.

And just as this flood was about to swamp me into its genetic current, I felt myself yanked up and *out*.

Rescued.

It happened at the Upper Room.

❧❧❧

"You need to come, Eric."

Lisa was beaming after an evening at a Cleansing

UNMASKED

Stream meeting at our new church, the Upper Room Fellowship Church. Butch, a friend who had been there with me through Phil's death, had been after me, too. And Pastor Kenny. And my daughter's pleading eyes pulled at my heartstrings. I knew I had to go, for her sake. It wasn't fair to ask her to battle those generational curses alone. I am her daddy, her protector, and it was time to pull myself up by my bootstraps and be all of what God called me to be.

༄༄༄

God don't make no junk.

It was the first truth that sunk into my thick skull at Cleansing Stream. As I sat with others in a small group, most as screwed-up as me, I realized that God had kept this appointment with me so that I could learn how to relate to him — in the company of trusted friends and family.

Everything in our world tends toward chaos without Jesus.

I considered how cars parked in storage rusted away, unless they were maintained. My father's 60-year-old body had wasted away due to cancer. My brother's mind fell victim to unmanageable depression and death. Mine would do the same ... if I refused to yield to God. Jesus was the only answer to this undeniable progression of chaos in the world.

God always provides a way of escape.

CORE VALUE

When I gave up my selfishness to Jesus, he gave me power over my thoughts. I no longer felt like a slave to the fiendish things that appeared on the screen of my brain. I had two sources that caused my thoughts: my own head and the author of selfishness, a spiritual person, who hankered to wipe me off the map. Most folks call him the devil.

Every demeaning thought in my head had a polar opposite, and each healing "opposite" was a gold nugget for the taking in the pages of God's word, the Bible. Suddenly, for me, it wasn't a matter of choice — this lifestyle became my survival.

I had the ability to scrub out generations of chaos that my ancestors chucked into my psyche as a child. My genetic makeup wasn't an issue anymore; Jesus bled and died to reverse my predictable "illnesses" of heart and mind, and his words healed me *moment by moment* as I forgave people and gave every detail of my life to God.

༄༄༄

Nowadays, after I repair an engine, the owner takes his car for a spin to make sure it's running according to the mechanic's promise — and that's what I did right after Cleansing Stream. I read God's word and applied every life example to my own situation. Every worry or bitter thought that entered my mind I rejected outright and then replaced the thought with the truth of what God said in the Bible — *about me.*

UNMASKED

It's amazing how my marriage has grown precious. How my job is easier to handle. How my daughter's health has improved. How I don't even think of blaming God for problems anymore; I refuse to let the originator of chaos ruin my day.

Hard questions.

I can't answer them all as leader of our men's ministry at the Upper Room, but God does in his time. I study God's word for *me,* and the overflow touches the hearts of those I talk to. I prod some of our hard cases toward Cleansing Stream sometimes, where no one gets an overhaul with "used" parts.

Instead they get a totally new "core" upon which God lovingly assembles every detail of their lives.

Healing relationships.

Mason, my handicapped brother, now lives in a special home in the Great Plains of Texas, beyond my care, but in God's capable hands. Mama is in heaven with Dad now, living in her new "mansion" where Jesus has healed her mind completely.

Phil's tragic life and death traumatized all of us who loved him, but most of all, his own children. Yet, in Phil's passing, God's determined love is renewing our troubled kin. Phil's daughter, whom he gave up for adoption as a toddler, is reaching out to us after years of uncomfortable silence. We pray that sharing our lives with my niece is the "trickle" before a river of God's blessing soaks our whole family with new health of mind and heart — especially Phil's kids.

CORE VALUE

And my personal miracle in all of this: God is restoring our family legacy for my daughter and her children in years to come.

ATTACKED
The Story of Kenny Martin, III
Written by Karen Koczwara

I felt it, slow and subtle at first, a steady rocking. Too terrified to open my eyes, I lay perfectly still, hoping it was my imagination. But then I felt it again, harder this time. This was not a bad dream. This was happening now.

In my bedroom.

In the middle of the night.

To me.

With my eyes squeezed shut, I lay frozen on my bed, praying that whatever or whoever it was would leave me alone. Hadn't I already endured enough?

The rocking grew stronger; it was as if two pairs of strange hands had grabbed hold of each side of my bed and were shaking it. Taunting me. Terrorizing me.

And then those terrible hands reached up with sharp claws and raked themselves up the side of my legs, grabbed me and instantly let go. It happened so quickly I wondered if it had been real. But my pulsing heart and trembling hands told me the truth.

This was very, very real.

Too terrified to open my eyes, I remained still, imagining the horrible, ugly creature peering down at me with a nasty sneer.

Never had darkness been so frightening. I lay there,

waiting for it to spring its claws again, but there was only silence now.

I was alone again.

Or was I?

❧❧❧

Less than an hour outside of the bustling city of Houston, Texas, sits the little town of Magnolia. Once a sleepy little sawmill community, it now boasts just more than 1,000 people, including retirees, families and businessmen. With acres of horse property and thick pine forests, it serves as the perfect place for a young boy to explore the outdoors. My family moved to Magnolia from Houston when I was in the first grade, trading high-rise buildings and noisy traffic for sprawling country land. Soon after we moved, we added six horses and two dogs to those green pastures. Property was cheaper on the outskirts of the city, and at last we could own a nice house.

The new five-bedroom two-story house we bought was an extension of that outdoor paradise. My older sister, Jennifer, made her room upstairs right across the hall from mine, while my younger brother, Will, claimed the one just down the hall. I enjoyed the space all to myself, yet if I needed something, my siblings were just an earshot away.

Little did I know that the bedroom I called my escape would soon be the very place my nightmare would begin.

ATTACKED

Our family was close; we spent our Friday nights munching on pizza, watching movies and playing games in the large bonus room upstairs. My father was a police officer and served with the Peace Officers during his spare time. He often talked about becoming a pastor of a church. My brother, sister and I spent our Sundays in church from the time we were born. I liked church, but I made up my mind as a little boy that I'd never be a pastor myself. From what little I knew, there seemed to be no money in that job.

From the time I was young, I had a difficult time falling asleep. Sometimes I lay awake for hours, staring at the ceiling in the dark as my mind replayed the day's events like a broken record. When at last I did fall asleep, I slept fitfully, often waking in the middle of the night and tossing and turning before drifting off again.

But when I was 9 years old, something strange happened.

As I lay awake one night, restless as usual, I heard hushed whispers coming from somewhere in the room. I slowly sat up in bed, musing that my fatigue must really be getting the best of me tonight.

"Will? Jennifer?" I called out in a small voice. But as I rubbed my eyes and the images in the room became clearer, I realized, to my horror, that the only person in the room was me.

I lay back down and tried to fall asleep, but the whispers began again, this time louder.

What on earth is going on? I pulled the covers up to

UNMASKED

my chin and closed my eyes. Surely, I must be imagining things. *There is no one in the room!*

A few nights later, as I tossed and turned on my bed, I heard the whispers again. The voices were indistinct; it was hard to tell if they were male or female or what they were saying. Terrified, I pulled the covers up against my chin again and closed my eyes tight. *Is this house haunted?* No, that's nonsense.

But what else could it be?

❧❧❧

As the months marched on, nighttime became my worst enemy.

"Okay, Kenny, finish your homework, and get upstairs for bed!" my mom called out after a late dinner one night.

I drug my feet down the hall and reluctantly climbed into bed. Within a few minutes after turning off the light, the whispers started again. I was beginning to feel a bit crazy. I thought about telling my brother and sister or parents but decided against it. They'd probably tell me I was just imagining things and that I needed to stop watching scary movies.

"Stop, go away!" I whispered into the dark, my stomach churning in knots as I lay perfectly still. Suddenly, a picture frame flew off the wall and landed with a thud on the ground. I jumped up, my heart racing, as I dared to look across the room. Earthquakes in Texas were about as common as hurricanes in Los Angeles;

ATTACKED

surely that hadn't been it. But how could something just fall off the wall?

With shaky legs, I climbed out of bed and picked up the picture frame with trembling hands. It was still in one piece, but I was a wreck. I tossed it onto my desk and ran back to bed, half expecting something to chase me under the covers. Voices were one thing, but this was downright scary.

That same year, I said a prayer and asked Jesus to come into my heart as my Savior and friend. My father explained that God loved us so much that he sent his son, Jesus, to come to earth and die on the cross for the wrong things we'd done. If we asked him into our heart, we could have a relationship with him and spend the rest of our lives with him in heaven.

"Would you like to get baptized?" my father prodded after we prayed. "It's a way to show the world that you believe in Jesus."

"Yes," I agreed heartily. I still had many things to understand about God, but since my father made a relationship with the Lord seem so inviting, I wanted that, too.

I got baptized shortly after making my decision; I knew my father was proud. "Maybe one day you will be called to serve others in the church, too," he said. He had begun a position as an interim pastor at a local church; it was a stretch financially for our family, but he was now doing what he knew was right for him.

"Maybe," I replied nonchalantly. *I hope not,* I added to

myself. *I don't want to be broke like every pastor I know, scrimping and saving pennies and eating leftovers every night. I want to move to the city and find myself a good job, a real job, someday.*

I threw myself into church, sports and school the next couple of years and enjoyed all three. Football was my favorite sport, and running track was a close second. Since I seemed to be athletically inclined, I wondered if I might be able to snag a college scholarship someday. As I raced around the field, my tennis shoes pounding the ground, I tried to forget about the terror that awaited me at home.

But forgetting about it did not make it go away.

One night, just after I'd turned off the lights, the fan in my room suddenly turned on. I dared to open my eyes and watched as it whirred around and around, blowing a steady breeze my way. I knew with certainty that I hadn't flipped the "on" switch. Shuddering, I jumped up to turn it off and climbed back into bed. I tried to fall asleep, but instead I tossed and turned, wracked with uneasiness, my fists clenched tightly, as though waiting for something to happen again. How could I sleep when something appeared to be after me?

One afternoon, I went to retrieve something in the attic upstairs. I sauntered into my brother's room and tried to open the wooden door leading to the attic. As I turned the doorknob, someone or something banged on the other side of the door three times. Startled, I jumped back and let go of the doorknob.

ATTACKED

"Who's there?" I croaked, my throat going dry. Maybe one of my siblings was playing a joke on me.

When no one replied, I ran out of the room and raced down the stairs.

"What's wrong?" my mother asked as she pulled the dinner out of the oven. "You okay?"

"Fine," I mumbled. "Have you seen Will and Jennifer?"

"They're out for the afternoon, remember?" she replied, staring at me oddly.

"Right." I realized my heart was thumping wildly in my chest. This just had to stop! I was starting to think I was losing my mind. I thought again about confiding in my mother, but I knew she'd just think I was imagining things.

Better to keep it to myself.

༺༻

As I entered high school, my heart began a tug-of-war game. Deep down, I knew God might be calling me to do some sort of work for him, but I didn't want to believe it was true. I had seen my parents struggle financially over the past few years after my father took a full-time job as a youth pastor at a Baptist church. Since the pay was meager, he worked two other jobs to make ends meet. I was beginning to think that being a pastor seemed like a whole lot of hard work for not very much pay. Plus, being a pastor's kid was beginning to get old. Kids at school and

UNMASKED

church expected us to have the perfect family, to have it all together all of the time.

"Your dad must be so great," they often said. "How cool it must be to be the pastor's kid!"

I loved my father, and he was a good pastor, but our home was far from perfect. I wished everyone would stop putting him on a pedestal and realize that we were an average, flawed family, just like all the rest of the folks in town.

I continued running track and playing football throughout high school and became known as a "jock" around campus. Popularity soon came my way, and I enjoyed the attention. When I won a track event and broke the standing record, my popularity soared even more. Soon, the invites to the parties started pouring in.

"So you'll be there Friday night?" my friend asked as we grabbed our football gear out of our locker one afternoon.

"Yeah, for sure." *Forget this pastor's kid image,* I thought to myself. *I'm going to have a little fun.*

I showed up at that party Friday night and had a few drinks. When a friend handed me a joint, I grabbed it and took a hit. The smoke burned my lungs a bit, but I took another, and slowly, a nice buzz settled in. *A little pot here and there can't really hurt,* I reasoned. *I'm not a bad kid; I'm just experimenting with the world.*

While I jumped back and forth between the good kid at church and the fun kid on Friday night, the nightmare

ATTACKED

in my bedroom continued. I was no longer a little boy, but I was still terribly afraid of the dark, and morning could never come soon enough.

During my sophomore year, something even stranger and unexplainable happened. As I stepped into the shower one morning, I looked down and recoiled in shock when I saw deep red scrapes up and down my legs. Though they were not bleeding, they burned terribly, as though someone had set my legs on fire. Despite getting tumbled a bit on the football field, I knew there was no way I could have done something like this to myself.

But if I didn't do it, where on earth did they come from?

Gingerly, I grabbed a tissue and tried to dab at the scrapes; they only burned more. Was it possible I'd been attacked in the middle of the night? Wouldn't I have woken up in pain, though? I shuddered as I turned on the shower and let the warm water run down my legs. I wanted this horrible experience to end once and for all. What had I done to warrant this? I wasn't a bad kid!

And then one night, something even more horrific took place. I had just settled into bed and dozed off when I felt the bed rocking back and forth. Too frightened to open my eyes, I lay there, frozen in fear. The rocking grew stronger, as though something on each side had taken hold of the bed frame and was shaking it with its hands. Then, out of nowhere, what felt like claws or sharp nails dug into my skin, raked my legs, grabbed me hard and then instantly released me.

UNMASKED

It was all I could do not to scream and run for my life.

I remained frozen, still too terrified to open my eyes, afraid that if I did, some horrific monster with sharp, gnashing teeth would be staring down at me. My heart raced so wildly I was certain it might jump out of my chest. As the adrenaline drained, I grew weak, feeling as if a semi-truck had run me over. Why was this happening to me? What was torturing me, and what did it want? I had become a prisoner in my own bedroom, and I could not take it anymore!

When my heart rate finally slowed and drowsiness overcame the awful images in my mind, I managed to fall into a restless sleep. And when morning came, I breathed a huge sigh of relief and headed off to school. Little did my family and peers know that I'd just experienced the most frightening night of my life.

My father had taken a job as an interim pastor at a small church in town. Unlike my Baptist church growing up, this church spoke about the powerful infilling of the Holy Spirit. God, the members of the congregation explained, could speak to us through the Holy Spirit. In return, we could gain greater access to him by inviting more of the Holy Spirit into our lives. I had never heard such terms used before.

"We have great power in Christ Jesus," an elderly lady told me one Sunday after church. "If we are troubled with something, we can pray and say, 'In Jesus' name,' and that spirit of trouble will leave us. There is another realm, you know, the spiritual realm. It is one we cannot see, but it is

ATTACKED

still very real. Demons are part of that realm, and like the devil, they want to discourage us from following Christ. They can be powerful, but the power we have in Jesus is even greater. If you are in trouble, just call on him."

A huge wave of relief surged through me at her words. For the first time, I realized that what I had been experiencing for the past several years was clearly a demonic attack. It was frightening to think about, but it was also tremendously encouraging to know that I did not have to keep enduring this nightmare. I could simply pray in Jesus' name and tell those demons to flee.

That night, as I climbed into bed, I shouted out, "In the name of Jesus, go!" I fell asleep in peace that night, and when I awoke at 3 a.m., I saw a beautiful bright light hovering just outside of my window. I could see just a sliver of it from between my broken window blinds, but as I peered closer, I knew just what it was: Jesus had sent an angel to watch over me!

"Thank you, Lord," I whispered. "You are real, and I know you are protecting me."

The following week, I ran after the elderly lady at church to ask her more about this thing she called spiritual warfare. "Anoint your room with oil, and pray over it," she explained. "And if you have anything that might displease the Lord, whether it be bad music or movies or books, get rid of those immediately. Don't leave any room for Satan."

I might once have thought this was crazy talk, but it suddenly all made so much sense. Satan wanted to defeat

UNMASKED

me, so he'd sent his demons to torture and taunt me. But I had a power greater than him; I had the Lord on my side. God could win this battle for me. I did not have to play the game anymore.

That night, I went home, anointed my room with oil as the wise lady had instructed and then sifted through all my books and movies. I pulled several out, knowing in my heart that the material was offensive to God. I had lived many years "on the fence," hopping from one side to the other in hopes that I could enjoy the best of both worlds. But in doing so, I hadn't truly surrendered myself to God and allowed him to use me. Smoking pot and drinking occasionally had once seemed like no big deal, but I now realized they were another way that Satan could sneak into my life and try to win me over to his side. If I wanted to be completely sold out to Christ, I had to stop compromising once and for all.

As I tried to fall asleep that night, I heard a shuffling in my room. My first reaction was fear, but I quickly remembered what I had learned. "In Jesus' name, flee!" I called out. Immediately, the noise stopped. I breathed a sigh of relief and lay back down.

"Thank you, God," I whispered into the dark.

I repeated my words, "In the name of Jesus, flee!" for the next several nights. And then, a wonderful and glorious thing happened. The strange noises and occurrences disappeared altogether. I could now sleep in peace because I had the power of Jesus on my side.

I told my parents about my experiences shortly after.

ATTACKED

"I can't believe you never told us this before, Kenny!" my mother cried, shaking her head in disbelief. "I'm so sorry you had to endure that all of these years. How terrible it must have been for you!"

"It was," I confessed. "But I don't live in fear anymore. I now know I have the power in Christ to defeat anything Satan tries to throw my way." I felt relieved to have my "secret" out in the open. Perhaps one day God would use my experience for good as I shared my story with others.

From that moment on, I turned my life completely around. I began leading Bible studies at school and joined the Fellowship of Christian Athletes. I wanted my peers to know that being a jock would not stop me from following Christ.

One day, as I read my Bible between classes, a fellow teammate stopped to say hello. "What are you reading there?" he asked.

"My Bible."

"Oh, so are you one of those Jesus freaks now?" he asked, raising his brow.

"Maybe," I replied with a wry smile.

Finally, I shared my story at a small group Bible study one night. "I thought the nightmare would never end, but I finally realized it was spiritual warfare. Once I did, I was able to call out in Jesus' name and boy, did that ol' devil take off like the wind!" I opened up my Bible. "It says here in John 4:4, 'You, dear children, are from God and have overcome them, because the one who is in you is greater than the one who is in the world.' Satan is the one who is in the world, and I'm sitting here tonight to tell you that this stuff is real. We live every day in a battle, but Christ is greater than Satan, and we can conquer Satan if we call out to Jesus for strength."

Though I was serving God in many capacities, I was still not convinced that going into ministry full time was really what he wanted me to do. With my future a blank canvas before me after high school graduation, I decided to enroll in the graphic design program at Sam Houston State University. I'd always been interested in graphic design, and it seemed the money wasn't too bad, either. I put my call to ministry on the back burner and threw myself into my new classes.

I can always go to seminary someday, down the line, I told myself.

But, just like Jonah in the Bible, who'd tried running from God and wound up in the belly of a whale, I soon realized that I could not run forever from my true calling. When I discovered that the music minister at my father's church back in Magnolia had left, I felt God nudging at my heart again. *Kenny, this is what I've made you to do,* he said.

An avid guitar player, I had always loved worship music. I prayed about it and decided it was time to head back to the little town of Magnolia and embrace my calling as a servant at the Upper Room Fellowship Church, where my dad was now the pastor.

The first Sunday I got up to play my acoustic guitar before the congregation, I felt both humbled and excited. I

ATTACKED

thought for a moment about those horrible nights I'd endured all those years and how God had released me from them. I could now see it all clearly. He had called me to ministry since I was a young boy, but I had resisted that call for some time. Satan had tried to snuff me out and pull me back into the world, but ultimately, his meager powers were no match for my Almighty God's. Ultimately, Satan lost out, and I could fulfill the purpose God had created me for.

It was so freeing to realize I had that power in Christ.

As I got to know people in the Upper Room Fellowship, I was impressed with their servants' hearts, eagerness for God and their generosity. Many had never set foot in a church before but found ours to be a safe place where they could truly let their hair down and be themselves.

ঞ্চঞ্চঞ্চ

"I heard you have a single mother in need." A woman approached me one Sunday morning. "I'd love to put a fundraiser together to help her out."

"That's a great idea," I agreed. Despite tough economic times, so many in our little church reached out to help others, giving what little they had to someone else who needed it more. What a good reminder to me that money had nothing to do with being fulfilled. Sharing each other's burdens was just one of the many reasons I looked forward to gathering with my friends every Sunday.

UNMASKED

As I lay down one night in bed, I pulled the covers over myself and thanked God that my restless nights were now behind me. The moonlight peeked through the window as I drifted off. I could now sleep peacefully, knowing that God watched over me in the darkness. I would not forget that every day was a spiritual battle. I would not let the devil try to destroy what God had meant for good. He was determined to drag me down, but I would stay on guard, and in the end, he wouldn't stand a chance.

My God will overtake *any* attack of the enemy.

REBEL RIDER
The Story of James Chase
Written by Arlene Showalter

"Go ahead," the Harley dealer said. "Hop on."

I swung my leg over the 1955 Harley Davidson 165 and passed a hand over the tank of the 2-year-old bike, admiring the still-fresh red and white paint. My fingers curled around the handlebars.

Perfect fit.

I clenched my jaw, determined to keep a tight rein on the excitement building deep in my gut. The Harley dealer counted every dollar I'd handed him — all $360 of it.

"She's yours, kid," Les Myers said. He waved the bills and grinned. "Enjoy."

I nodded, revved the engine and carefully swung the bike out onto the road before testing its pull. I hammered down, releasing the pent-up joy with a whoop.

The wind beat against pounds of hair grease, intended to keep my ducktail do intact, and scrubbed my face with heated fingers.

The bike's power vibrated from my legs, up through my torso and shook loose the deep sadness lodged in my broken heart. It tumbled to the ground like shattered pottery, and I crushed it into the road's graveled surface with the Harley's wheels.

I inhaled the heady mix of hot Texas air and Harley fumes and fell headlong into my first love affair — that of kid and machine. We bound ourselves to a common goal — the quest of untamed, nonconformist, unconventional freedom.

Our combined ages totaled 15.

Rippin' It Up

Would you be proud of me? I wondered as I studied the photo over the mantel. The serious-looking-dark-haired-sharp-eyed-full-blooded-Chickasaw-born-U.S. Army soldier stared back.

I heard Grandma bustling around her kitchen, preparing dinner for her men folk. Grandpa came in the back door, stomping field dirt from his boots.

"Mind your step," Grandma prompted.

"Smells good," returned Grandpa. He entered the living room and stood behind me.

"Whatcha thinkin', son?" he asked, his firm voice tinged in kindness.

"Nothing," I lied.

"You know, your father fought under General MacArthur," Grandpa explained. "In the Pacific, during World War II."

"Did he get him lotsa bad guys," I asked him, "before he …?"

"Yes," Grandpa said. "He beat 'em good. Your daddy was a sharpshooter. One of Uncle Sam's best." He paused. "Got his shootin' skills righ' chere in Texas. Could knock a horned toad off a rock at a hundred paces."

REBEL RIDER

"Time to eat!" Grandma called. "Wash up."

My grandparents had rejected the U.S. government's insistent offer to move onto a reservation, too proud to accept what they considered charity. Although Grandpa resented the American government's attempt to cage his people, he and Grandma decided to raise their brood of nine children in the white man's world, realizing reservation life held no future for him or his family.

Grandpa bought 100 acres just outside Wichita Falls, Texas, and taught each of his boys how to live off the land. However, one by one, they drifted away from the farm and into city life until, only I, his deceased son's son, remained.

The next morning Grandma called me at 5 a.m. to get up to do chores, as I did every morning during the summer break from school.

I measured feed for the horses and pondered what Grandma had told me.

"Geraldine's coming to visit."

I searched my memory, trying to recall my absent mother's face. My dad had married an Irish/English woman with a fondness for alcohol. When the call of duty took him off to war, my mother filled her empty days and arms with another man.

Her *Dear John* letter lay resting against his heart when an enemy bullet took him out.

I was 2 months old.

Grandpa took me from Geri, my mother, not long after my father's death, because guilt accelerated her already-beyond-saturated level of alcohol consumption.

UNMASKED

Now, years later, she was coming to visit *me*. I could hardly contain my excitement as I forked fresh hay into the horse's stalls.

The day finally came. I stared at the petite auburn-haired woman standing on our front porch.

"Hello, James." Her gentle voice caressed my 8-year-old ears, unaccustomed to its sound.

"Hi, Geri."

She smiled. "That's perfectly all right," she said, "to call me by name. Now," she stretched out a hand. "What shall we do for fun?"

"Want to see the horses?" I asked.

We examined the Texas prairie on horseback, swam in my favorite spots and explored a relationship. In one month, we progressed from curious strangers, to close friends, to just-a-hair shy of parent-child relationship.

"Do you have to go back to California?" I asked.

"For now," Geri said. "But I promise I'll come back as quick as I can."

A year later, she made good on her promise. She moved to Wichita Falls, found a new man, married and settled down.

Trouble Doubled

While maneuvering Grandpa's tractor across the fields, I saw Grandma come out of the house and stand on the back porch. She waved me in for dinner.

I waved back, parked the tractor and headed in. My

REBEL RIDER

11-year-old stomach growled its anticipation of Grandma's tasty cooking.

"I don't feel so well." Grandma set her fork down on the table and rubbed her leg. "My hip hurts."

Grandpa's brows knit.

"You want us to call the doc in to see you?"

"Yes, I believe so."

Grandpa's frown deepened.

Grandma never complains. I pulled my face out of my plate to study her face — pinched with pain. *This has gotta be serious.*

The doctor came and ordered bed rest.

"You must've pulled a muscle," he decided. "See that she obeys, son," he said, patting my shoulder as he passed.

Two days later, Grandpa's youngest son, Ken, and his wife sat with Grandpa and me in the kitchen, discussing Grandma's condition. A loud thud sent us racing to her room.

Grandma lay on the floor, next to the space heater she'd knocked over.

"Call the ambulance," Ken shouted as he bent over his mother.

"Mom, what do you think you're doing?" he asked, a smidge of tenderness creeping into the barked question.

"I had to go to the bathroom," she gasped.

The ambulance came, collected Grandma and screamed all the way to the hospital.

"She's had a stroke," the doctor intoned. I searched his face.

UNMASKED

She ain't gonna make it.
Affirmative.

As Grandpa and I drove to the little Baptist church for the funeral, winking Christmas lights seemed to taunt our loss. We pulled into the parking lot already filled with the cars of people determined to honor their quiet, faithful friend and neighbor.

My grandma.

"What will we do?" I asked Grandpa later as we sat, staring at nothing, in the kitchen. Its silent emptiness thundered in our ears and echoed through our vacant hearts.

"Don't know, son, but ..." Foreign tears traveled through the rivulets of his suntanned, normally inscrutable face. He swiped at them. "We'll be okay."

He tried hard to fill Grandma's apron, but stumbled about the house, like a greenhorn on a 10,000-acre spread, over the mysteries surrounding her domestic world of cooking and cleaning.

I spent more time with Geri and her husband, Andy. He owned a leatherworks shop and enjoyed teaching me how to build saddles and military footwear.

He treated me with the same respect he had for his craft. I appreciated that.

"Look here, James," he said, pride coloring his voice, as he caressed the toe of another finished boot. "These here boots go to soldiers all over the world."

My mind flashed back to my stranger-father, forever standing sentinel over his parents' mantle place. I busied

REBEL RIDER

my hands, polishing another handcrafted saddle, fashioned under Andy's skilled guidance. *I wonder if he'd be proud of me now.*

I respected Andy and loved Geri, but her taste for alcohol soured their relationship. The constant bickering led to chronic depression in Geri.

"James, I just wish I was dead," she moaned on more than one occasion.

❧❧❧

Some friends and I headed out for a party, six months after Grandma's death.

"Hey, guys," I said, as we neared Geri's home, "let's stop for a minute so I can say hi to my mom."

"Okay," they agreed.

We pulled up the driveway.

Geri stepped out on the porch.

"Hi, James," she said. "Andy and I are fixing to go out."

"That's okay," I said. "We were passing by, and I just wanted to say hi."

We went on to the host's house. Hours later, as the party began to wind down, several of us drifted to the porch, enjoying the cool quiet of approaching midnight.

A siren blared in the distance.

"Here comes the heat," one guy snickered.

"Yep, they're after you, for sure," another joked.

"I'd better get going," I said. "It's late."

UNMASKED

"Don't let them cops nab you," the guys ordered.
I laughed and left for home and bed.

"What … what?" I sat up, rubbing my eyes. Something, someone was shaking me.

"Wake up, James." Geri's brother stood over me. "Your mom's in the hospital."

"Geri … hospital?" My brain fought for wakefulness. The clock's hands stood frozen at 2 a.m.

"Just come on," he barked. "Hurry!"

Andy and the doctor met us at the door of Geri's room. Andy's eyes told it all.

She's gone. My brain whirled. *How? Why?*

We turned to Andy. He shrugged, weeping openly.

"I don't know why," he blubbered. "I don't. We went out and had a good time. When we got back …" He stopped to wipe his eyes. "I went to take a shower." He stopped again, gulping for air.

"I heard the shot from the shower and ran down the hall." His eyes closed against the memory. "Geri lay on … on our … our bed, the gun still in her hand."

That one bullet shattered my world. At 13, I'd lost the two most important women in my life.

Purpose died.

Desolation conquered love.

Obliterated it.

I cut classes and relationships and started hanging out with older, badder guys. Guys who owned Harleys and — in my young eyes — ruled the world.

REBEL RIDER

I set my heart on owning my own bike — a Harley like what my new friends owned. I begged Grandpa to let me get a job. He agreed.

I landed a job, the summer of my 13th year, washing wine, martini and whiskey glasses at Abe Lincoln's bar, earning 30 cents an hour. The goal kept my hands busy and my mind focused.

Bikers are tight folk. They watch one another's backs. I was running short on family and felt a desperate need to find some.

My aunts and uncles, legally my brothers and sisters since my adoption at age 4, hated me.

"I oughta throw you out here," my older uncle/brother often snarled, while driving past Geri's house, before my mom's death. "You belong with that two-timing-husband-killing b****."

I'll show you. My jaw tightened. *I'll show you all.*

That Harley bike transported me, at 13, into a life of untamed freedom. I straddled its power and started riding with a pack of guys.

We called ourselves the Kickapoo Cowboys, taking the name from a lake north of town. School and farm chores receded from the horizon of my conscious mind.

"I'm going to have to fail you," the principal told me at the end of seventh grade. "You're missing too much school."

I shrugged. I had my bike. I was King of the Road in my own eyes.

Who needs an education?

UNMASKED

Grandpa couldn't keep up with 100 acres, farm animals, untended house and one wild grandson.

Meanwhile, I racked up an impressive amount of "coupons": speeding tickets, operating a motor vehicle without a license citations and dodging the heat.

"I'm telling you boys," Sheriff Vance scolded one day as the Kickapoo Cowboys hung out at the local Triumph cycle shop. We'd hidden our bikes behind the building and sat around, each looking as innocent as a feline with a mouth full of canary carcass.

"I might not be able to catch you boys on those fancy bikes," he warned, "but let me assure you, I *will* shoot you off them someday."

I grinned. His threats hung impotent in the charged atmosphere. Grandpa hated him, and he knew it.

At 4, I'd sat next to Grandpa on his porch. Sheriff Vance drove up and parked his squad car. Geri had stepped out onto the sidewalk.

"Ira," the sheriff had begun, placing a boot on the bottom step. "I've come for the kid."

"You touch that boy, Vance," Grandpa hefted the claw hammer in his hand, "I'll beat you with this."

The sheriff dropped his foot back to the sidewalk.

"Now, get off my property." Grandpa half rose from his chair. Sheriff Vance and Geri retreated.

One week later, the county awarded my grandparents permanent custody, via adoption.

REBEL RIDER

Against the Wind

I roared through life, existing, non-existing, barely existing, for the next three years.

"You need to go into the Army, son," Grandpa advised. "And get yourself an education."

Yeah, and get out of this mess, I thought later as I walked through downtown. I approached the Navy recruiter's office and, without thinking, stepped in.

"I want to enlist," I said, "but I'm only 16."

"No problem," the officer said. "Navy's got a new program. If your parents will sign for you, you can enlist as a Reservist now and go active at 17."

I looked over his neat blue uniform. *This town's got nothing to offer me,* I thought. *I'm gonna go for it.*

I sped home.

"Grandpa, will you sign for me to enlist in the Navy?" I asked the moment I burst into the house.

He studied me. "That's what you're wanting, son?" he asked.

"Yes, sir," I replied.

Grandpa signed.

I enlisted.

Bad to the Bone

The Navy shipped me 400 miles south to Galveston, Texas, and put me out to sea on a destroyer for two weeks. I stood on the deck, sensing the ocean's power beneath me

UNMASKED

and inhaling its scent for the first time in my life. Its breezy saltiness thrilled me. I licked my lips, sampled its saline seasoning — and fell in love.

The Navy returned me to land and the status of a bored reservist. *I can't take this,* I thought, making my way to the Yeoman's office.

"What do I have to do to go active?" I asked.

"You want action?" he asked.

"Yes, sir."

"Just quit coming to the meetings. You'll get action."

I followed orders, and in no time, a parole officer pounded on my door.

"You are to report for active duty," he barked.

"Yes, sir!"

The Navy assigned me to another destroyer, the USS *Bradford*, bound for her final voyage to Bremerton, Washington, where she would become a decommissioned vessel.

I trained as a sport diver, loving the rush of man against water.

I returned to San Diego, now assigned to a destroyer tender, the USS *Grand Prairie*. Destroyers are built to protect larger ships, such as aircraft carriers, traveling in fleets. Tenders maintain the destroyers. We docked at Pier 6, at 32nd Street Naval Station, principal homeport for the U.S. Pacific Fleet.

One night, while reading a magazine, I saw an article about the Navy searching for volunteers to train as repair divers.

REBEL RIDER

I put in my request and got accepted.

After intensive training, my fellow divers and I stood in perfect formation, waiting to receive our diving certificates. The base commandant strode into the room.

"Sailors," he said, "the Navy's got a new program, approved by the Commander in Chief himself, President Kennedy."

I stood taller.

"This is going to be the most challenging job in the entire Navy," he continued. "So, it's *volunteers only* for this specialized training."

He looked us over. "You boys take a year to think on it," he advised.

I looked straight at the commandant and stepped forward. "Sir," I said, "I want to volunteer right now."

The other 11 graduates joined me. "And I," each echoed.

"You boys sure?" he asked.

"Yes, sir," we chorused, as one.

He stood in front of me.

"You got a high school diploma, sailor?" he barked.

"No, sir."

"You've got exactly two weeks to acquire one."

I studied, crammed, memorized — and passed.

The testing took four days. We studied one subject for a whole day, took an exam and passed on to the next subject. I stared at the final report and grinned. *This good ol' farm boy, who barely squeaked by the eighth grade, just passed himself with a B+.*

UNMASKED

I was on my way to bigger and better things, and I knew it.

I entered the UDT, or Underwater Demolition Team, training as part of the new Navy SEAL (Sea-Air-Land) program. The intense training prepared us to fight anywhere, at any time and by any means necessary to accomplish whatever mission the commander ordered.

☙☙☙

"You soldiers hungry?" our instructor shouted over the brisk March wind as we stood on a North Island pier.

"Yes, sir!" we shouted back.

"Good." He gestured across the San Diego Bay. "It's over there, and you're swimming to it."

I plunged into the 58-degree water, clenching my teeth against its callous chill, and battled the seven-knot current. *You'll never amount to anything.* My uncle/brothers' words echoed through my freezing body. Their taunts propelled me forward, stroke by endless stroke, until my fingers brushed the pier — on the other side.

Victory pulsated life back into my numbed body — one staccato beat at a time.

"Hell Week" came. Our instructors pushed us with training exercises for a continuous 132-hour period, allowing a mere four hours of sleep per night, taxing our mental and physical strength to the point of emotional implosion.

REBEL RIDER

I heard the officers' taunts through the haze of extreme exhaustion. "Just ring the bell thrice, and you can go to a nice place, have a bath, good food, beer and some sleep."

Ringing the bell equaled DOR, or drop-on-request. *Not me.* I gritted my teeth, placing one beat foot in front of the other. *Grandpa didn't raise him no quitter.*

We graduated, the third unit to do so in the new SEAL program, and stood — eight strong, proud young men — feeling 10 feet tall and bulletproof.

"Congratulations, soldiers," President Johnson said. "You are now the finest killing machines the world has ever known." My chest inflated over his words.

"We are depending on your skills to win the war," LBJ continued. Adrenaline surged through my 19-year-old body. *I made it.* I struggled to control the raging triumph I felt. *I showed them! None of Grandpa's kids ever met a president, let alone shake his hand.*

My father's face floated across the canvas of memory. *Would you be proud of me?*

We shipped out for Vietnam.

"Your mission is to go above the Demilitarized Zone, into Cambodia, and capture this VC general." Our commanding officer flashed the photo of the Viet Cong leader. "Your only weapons will be knives, teamwork and — your wits."

We slipped across the border, our hushed boots turned in the direction of our target. I peered into the bush, seeing nothing, hearing nothing.

"Your father was colorblind." Grandpa's words, from

UNMASKED

long ago, invaded my heightened awareness of silent, lurking danger. "Made him the best sniper on the squad," Grandpa bragged.

"How was that?" I'd asked.

"Didn't get distracted by color," Grandpa explained.

I could use your skill now, Dad.

We located our man, drugged and bound him and slipped back into Vietnam.

After we'd strapped him into a parachute harness, we strung a line between two trees and clipped him to it. A C-141 cargo plane lumbered low overhead, a hook dangling from a trip wire, attached to the vehicle's rear door. The hook snagged the line and jerked the trussed-up general skyward, shooting him from 0 to 180 knots — in one second flat.

On a later mission, I served as point man for my squad, walking ahead with a Vietnamese guide, to scout the bush. He led, while I studied the map.

"We go here," he said, pointing left, when we reached a fork in the path.

I looked at the map and scowled. "The map says right," I said.

"No, no." He shook his head. "This way right way."

"I'm not going that way," I argued. "The map says right."

We glared at each other, and then I turned and started down the path to the right.

A searing pain streaked through my right shoulder. Before I could respond, the guide had ripped out his spear and sunk it into my left shoulder and withdrew it again.

I whirled around. He pierced my knee. I grabbed the spear, holding it in place with one hand while the other closed around my knife. I snagged the flesh at his groin and ripped north, stopping only when I'd reached the point under his chin.

"How dare you try to kill me!" I screamed as our bloods converged, saturating the ground beneath us. "You'll never kill me. You ain't got the guts."

I stepped over his lifeless face and rejoined my team.

We took the right path.

Mad Max

I planned to make the Navy my career — until I escorted my best friend, Johnny, home in a body bag. *I just gotta get out of here — alive.*

I boarded the plane for my final trip stateside. My eight years netted me three Purple Hearts — and a fourth, made of stone.

I reported to the Brooklyn Naval Yard for my last six months of service.

There, I met Cathy, also serving in the U.S. Navy. I signed onto marriage with a military ceremony and three days later signed out of the service.

Nightmares haunted me. I turned to whiskey to tame them.

The Navy discharged Cathy on medical leave when she became pregnant with our first child.

UNMASKED

An unknown, unnamed restlessness kept me on the move, from job to job, town to town, state to state. No occupation or location satisfied me for long.

Nightmares waxed with time and waned with whiskey.

☙☙☙

"Grandpa." I called as the holidays approached. "I can't make it down for Christmas, but I promise I'll be there in July, for your birthday."

"Son, if you don't come now," Grandpa answered, "I'll never see my grandbabies."

Something in his voice moved me to pack up Cathy and the girls and drive from Pennsylvania to Texas.

A few days after our arrival, I was out in his yard with my girls, when Cathy appeared at the door.

"James," she said. "Your grandpa wants to see you — right now."

"Okay." I kept playing with the girls.

"Right now," she insisted. "It's urgent."

"What's the matter?" I asked as I stepped onto the porch.

"He's asking to go to the hospital."

"Hospital?" I echoed, pushing past Cathy and trotting to Grandpa's room.

He sat, bent over, on the side of the bed.

"What's wrong, Grandpa?" I asked. "Are you sick?"

"No, son, I ain't sick," he replied. "Just fixin' to die."

I stared at my still-strong-arrow-straight-92-year-old

grandfather. "Don't want to die in front of the kids, is all," he continued, his voice even. "Please take me to the hospital."

"You're not dying, Grandpa," I said.

He lifted his face to stare straight into my eyes. "Ever lied to you before, son?"

"No, sir."

"Then get your car, and help me to the hospital."

In the culture he'd left, an aging brave takes his blanket and weapons out into the woods and dies in solitary dignity. Not free to practice the custom in the white man's world, Grandpa opted for the next best choice — death, alone in a hospital.

He wafted out of life four hours later.

ಹಿಹಿಹಿ

My hands trembled as I rested them on the casket's open lid.

I stared down at this man who'd taught me to never back down, no matter what the odds.

In second grade, I had charged past him, sitting on the porch, and into the house.

"Boy, what're you running from?" he'd asked.

"Nothing, Grandpa." I tossed the words back, still on the run.

"Son," he hollered. "You bring me my razor strap — now." I returned, head hanging and strap dangling from my fingers.

UNMASKED

"Now," he said, "no more lies. What you running from?"

"That new kid in school, Butch, said he wuz gonna whup me," I explained. "With two of his friends."

"Go get your work clothes on," Grandpa ordered.

I looked in his eyes, turned and obeyed.

As soon as I'd changed, Grandpa guided me onto the road back to the school.

"Why are we going back?" I asked.

"Because you are going to fight them boys," he said.

"All three?" I asked.

"Yes."

"They'll pound me," I whined.

"No, they ain't."

When we arrived at the school, I pointed out the trio, with great reluctance. Grandpa marched me over and directed me to fight them, one by one. I did and won — three times.

After we returned home, Butch's daddy came calling.

"What's this about you making your kid fight mine?" he'd snarled at Grandpa.

"Did your boy tell you that him and his buddies were ganging up on my boy?"

"No," Butch's daddy admitted.

"Well, I made James fight them boys, one at a time," Grandpa declared. "I'm teaching my boy not to back down — for anyone or anything."

"Gotcha." Butch's dad had nodded.

Then he said, "Don't you worry none about my son.

REBEL RIDER

I'll whip him myself when I get back home. He won't bother your boy no more."

The memory faded while I continued to search the still face of this man who'd reared me, taught me to face life and stand as a man.

My respect for him rose up and engulfed the profound sorrow choking me.

"Grandpa," I whispered, "I've never loved anyone as much as I've loved you."

The lid clicked shut. I left the funeral parlor, the homestead and Texas.

I never looked back.

I took a job driving truck long distance. It kept me from home and my increasingly unhappy wife, Cathy.

"I hate your drinking," she spat. "At home, on the road — everywhere and at any time."

I shrugged. "Truck don't start without whiskey."

Finally, she'd had enough. She found someone new, divorced me and moved herself and the girls 80 miles away.

Every other Friday, I drove over to pick up my girls. On one such weekend, I struggled to make it to Cathy's home after a big snowstorm. I finally arrived and pulled into the driveway. I climbed out of my truck, buttoning my thick parka, and knocked on the back storm door.

Cathy's boyfriend, Brink, appeared.

"Where's Cathy?"

"Shopping. She'll be back in a bit."

UNMASKED

"She knows it's my weekend to get the kids," I said. "Bring them out."

"Nope," he replied from the other side of the locked door. "You ain't getting them this weekend."

"Boy," I said, my anger rising, "I'm going to ask you one more time. Bring my kids out."

"Over my dead body," he sneered.

I catapulted myself through the glass door and yanked him outside. He resisted like a rag doll. I pummeled him into unconsciousness and left him lying, in his jeans and t-shirt, in the reddened snow.

I threw off my parka, stomped into the house, collected my kids and exited through the front door.

The phone rang all weekend. "Don't answer it," I ordered my new wife. "It's Cathy. I'm going to enjoy my kids. I'll talk to her when I take them back Sunday night."

When I parked in front of Cathy's house, I noticed the chief of police had pulled up behind my truck. I glanced his way as I ushered the girls into the house.

"You'll never see the kids again," Cathy snarled. "I can guarantee that."

"We'll see."

I left, walked over to the chief's cruiser and got in.

"Okay," I said. "You can take me to jail now. I'm ready to face the music."

"I'm not going to put you in jail," he said, "but you *do* have to get out of this county — and don't come back. The boyfriend's got 120 stitches holding him together. It's a wonder he's still breathing."

REBEL RIDER

"Nobody comes between me and my kids," I growled.

"I understand," he said, "but the truth is, if you return to this county, I *will* have to arrest you for assault."

I moved back to Texas and became an owner/operator truck driver. Familiar restlessness drove me on to Oklahoma for some years and then back to Texas again.

Drinking, Driving and Dancing

After Cathy's departure, life became a whirlwind of whiskey guzzling to empty my mind, driving over the road to fill my wallet and dancing with women to fill my arms. I haunted the bars and clubs, dancing the Texas two-step, eager to show off whatever lady I held in my arms that night, and searched for fights to display battle-readiness.

Money made drinking and dancing partners easy to find. We'd hitch up for a dance, two-step into acquaintance, promenade to relationship and spin out into splitsville.

Quick to drink. Quick to fight. Slow to love. Slow to forget.

I kept my heart of hearts secret and remote, distant and unknown.

Beautiful Back Warmer

"Hi, I'm James." I held my hand out to the pretty woman at the bar. "Would you like to dance?"

"Sure." She smiled up at me. "I'm Glenda. I'd love to."

UNMASKED

We stepped onto the dance floor. I drew her into my arms. Quick, quick, slow, slow. Quick, quick, slow, slow. We circled the highly polished wooden floor and two-stepped our way into each other's hearts.

Although Glenda and I met at a bar, she cared little for the drink and dance treadmill that so satisfied me.

"James," she said one Sunday morning, "I want to go back to church."

A new opportunity to show off my shiny new boots — and truck. "Sure, babe," I agreed.

"The drinking's out of hand." Her brows knit together. "Maybe church will help."

"Okay."

It was easy to quit drinking. I managed seven or eight times that year alone.

"You'd better slack off that stuff," Glenda warned as New Year's Eve approached.

"I'll be all right."

We'd invited one couple to celebrate with us. They planned to arrive at our house just before midnight.

I began nipping at the stash long before the time and passed out by 10 p.m.

Crash!

Survival instinct had me on my feet in a nanosecond, searching for the cause of the ruckus. Glenda stood in the kitchen, firing dishes into the sink with frightening precision.

"What are you doing?" I yelled.

"I told you to stop drinking!" she screamed back.

REBEL RIDER

"When Harl and Betty got here, you were snoring on the couch. They were so embarrassed, they excused themselves and left."

She fired another plate into the growing pile of debris. *Smash!*

"Honey, please stop," I begged. I tried to wrap my arms about her.

She twisted away, snagged another plate and lobbed it after its mates. *Blam!*

"I'm sorry," I said. "Please calm down. Please — can we talk?"

Glenda leaned against the refrigerator and folded her arms.

"Here's where I'm at, James." She snapped off each word like the rapid fire of a Stoner 63 machine gun. "You quit drinking or I'm leaving you."

I took one step forward. She held up a hand to halt my progress.

"You get drunk again and I'm going back to Oklahoma. I'll kiss you goodbye while you're sleeping it off, and I'll be gone."

I searched her eyes and saw the same determination shining in them as I had any of my SEAL comrades on a mission.

Glenda had ordered a task harder than any I'd faced in Nam. *Mission accomplished* came easy there. Here, in civilian life, I struggled with her ultimatum.

Five months later, I stared at the calendar. Fourth of July. I'd planned a huge party for all my truck driving

UNMASKED

buddies and their girls. I still struggled with the bottle, and so far, Glenda had not made good on her threat to leave.

I had the house fully stocked, lacking only a half-gallon of whiskey — and a fifth for my truck. *It still don't run without it.*

I parked at the liquor store, cut the engine and paused.

"God …" Moisture blurred my vision, and my heart throbbed with a fierce ache. "I want to quit drinking. I just don't know how."

I passed a hand over my eyes. "I need some help."

I climbed out of the truck and turned my feet toward the store.

Go to the phone booth.

"Huh?"

Go into the phone booth — there by the front door.

I obeyed the blast of the silent voice, stepped into the phone booth and closed the door.

"Now what?" I asked my unseen superior officer.

"Call your wife."

I dialed the number.

"Hello." Glenda's voice calmed me.

I opened my mouth, and the words that popped out shocked me like a 1,000-volt charge.

"Glenda, take every bottle of liquor in the house, and pour it down the sink," I instructed.

"Do what?" she gasped.

"I'm serious," I answered. "And take my monogrammed shaker, jump up and down on it until it can't shake another drink."

Glenda started crying. "You're serious?"

"As serious as I've ever been in my life, baby," I said. "Put some fresh flowers on the bar." I paused. "I don't know why I'm saying all this, but just do it." I paused again. "Please stop crying, baby. I can't take it. I'll be home soon."

I turned my back to the liquor store door, got into my truck and drove home.

Glenda met me at the door.

"Would you like a drink?" she asked, a smile lighting her beautiful face.

"Yes, I would," I answered. "A nice cup of coffee."

"I just made a pot," she responded.

"That sounds wonderful."

Three weeks later, we both rededicated our lives to God.

Ride Captain

Life changed for the better, but we still loved to dance and the best dances took place in clubs. Glenda and I frequented them, drinking cokes alongside our alcohol-consuming friends.

One night, while at a club, an on-duty-liquor-imbibing officer draped an arm around my wife. I removed his arm and him — in short order.

Hours later, I heard a truck approach our house. My gut told me the cop had come, off duty, to burn me. I hefted my shotgun in one hand and stepped out to where

UNMASKED

he was parked on the street. He flipped his lights on to blind me. Instinct brought the shotgun up, and I began blasting — each headlight first, then the front tires and finally the radiator. A screaming siren halted my effortless progress.

Glenda, fearing for my life, called the sheriff. A nearby highway patrolman had responded. He booked me on assault with intent to murder a police officer. A guilty verdict carried a mandatory sentence of life without parole.

"He's a former Navy SEAL," the attorney argued at sentencing. "He's trained for survival."

"I agree," the judge said, turning to me. "I'm giving you 25 years with chance of parole after 10."

"Glenda," I said, before they took me away, "if you want to divorce me, you go right ahead. I won't blame you. Ten to 25 years is too long to wait for anyone."

She shook her head, tears dropping from her face. "No. We're in this together."

I settled myself in the back of the squad car, hands shackled behind me. I bowed my head and heart.

"Lord," I prayed, "I'll never make it through this one without you."

చుచుచు

God stuck closer to me than my SEAL buddies during my prison stint. One night, while attending service at the prison chapel, the preacher stood to announce, "The Lord told me someone in this room is plagued by nightmares and an uneasy spirit. Whoever that person is, I want you to come up here right now so I can pray for you."

He's talking about you, James.

"I know, Lord." I stood up. Tears dotted my way up the aisle.

"Pastor, that's me," I said when I met him at the front. "I can't sleep. I have nightmares. I break into cold sweats."

I swiped at my wet eyes. "I have so much hatred in my heart. I just don't know how to get rid of it."

The pastor anointed me with oil and laid his hands on my head. "I command this force to leave you — now — and I bind it away from you and your life forever."

I sank to my knees.

"You are delivered of this sin, in the name of Jesus," he declared.

A lightness, an illumination, a dawning burst upward and out from my heart, while the weight of unforgiveness and hate dropped to the ground and melted away.

"Praise God, praise God!" I shouted. "I'm free at last!"

Master Chief

"I'm ready to go," I said, rapping on the locked kitchen door.

"Wait," the officer on the other side commanded.

Wait? I never had to wait before. The prison had promoted me to trustee status, which meant the guards never searched my person or questioned my requests.

UNMASKED

I rapped on the door again. *I must've heard him wrong,* I decided.

"I told you to wait," the officer snapped.

The old anger rose up, wrapped itself like a boa around my heart and pulsated through to my clenched fists.

Lord, I don't know what's going on, I prayed, *but I need you to control this anger.*

Fifteen minutes later, the guard unlocked and opened the door. I stepped into the hallway and choked down a gasp. The walls were lined with men, some bleeding, and all shackled.

Prison fight.

Had the guard opened that door at my first knock, I'd have been in it, voluntarily or not.

See, I told you I would take care of you, I heard the Lord's voice say, deep within me.

"You always do," I agreed. "You always do."

The years crawled by. Glenda came down from Oklahoma at least once a month for visitation. God continued to walk with me and protect me.

Nine years into my incarceration, a guard who'd befriended me approached me in the rec yard.

"I need to talk to you."

"Sure," I said. "What's up?"

"Gary called," he said, referring to a former inmate. He handed me a cigarette. "Got some tough news for you."

We became friends. After Gary's release, Glenda stayed with his wife and him when she flew to Texas to visit me.

REBEL RIDER

"About what?"

"Can't tell you. It's gonna be a shock for you. I want you to know I'm here for you."

He led me to his office, dialed Gary's number and handed me the phone.

"Hey, Gary," I said, when he answered. "What's going on?"

"Don't know how to tell you this, James." He cleared his throat. "Glenda passed away today."

I sat down, hard. Shock staggered my mind. I felt my world crumble to dust beneath my prison-issue boots.

"How? Why?"

"Aneurysm," Gary said. "She'd been complaining of headaches, but thought nothing of it."

I returned to my cubicle on autopilot. "What do I do now, God?" I prayed. "Parole won't let me move out of state."

The prison "graciously" housed me for an extra year because I had no place to go.

"God, I know your word is true. I know that everything happens for good … only I can't see the good of this at the moment," I told God months later. "You promised never to leave me, and I still trust you on that."

I clung harder to God because — I had no place else to go.

After choir practice that night, a buddy followed me to my cubicle.

"Want me to pray for you, James?" he asked.

"Sure," I agreed. "I never turn down prayer."

UNMASKED

He leaned against the door frame. "I've been asking God what words to give you to comfort you." He paused. "Look me in the eye, James, because you're not going to like what I have to say."

I raised my head — and waited.

"The Lord told me that if you had gone back to Oklahoma, you'd have fallen back into your old ways. He had to protect you so that you could be faithful to his service."

I didn't argue with him, but neither did I understand the message.

More months passed. Then I got a letter from a chaplain in another unit.

Dear James,

I understand your wife passed away, and you've no place to go when you are released. An employee is leaving my company in Houston, and I'll keep his job open for you. If you want it, just call me when you get out. P.S. I have a place for you to stay, too.

Chaplain Moore

Before my release, I was participating with several other men in a prayer circle. One guy, who'd never met me, led off in prayer. In the middle of it, he stopped, looked straight at me and said, "James, the Lord just told me you are going to minister to people just like you." He then resumed his prayer.

REBEL RIDER

The prison released me on a Thursday.

The next day I received a phone call from my buddy, Tom.

"James, how about joining us in a prison ministry?" he asked.

"You know the rules," I said. "I can't go anywhere near a prison for two years."

"Okay," he said. "I'll pick you up for church on Sunday. Be ready at 8 a.m."

"Sure."

Sunday came. "We're going to Beaumont," Tom announced.

"Why Beaumont?" I asked.

"Going to the prison," he replied.

"Now, Tom, I told you I can't go in there for two years," I protested.

"Save it." Tom grinned. "I talked to the warden. You're in."

ॐॐॐ

Four months after my release, I sat in the door of my camper, where I lived on the job, working as weekend guard, sipping coffee, alone and lonely.

Lord, I prayed. *If it's okay with you, could you send me a girl? Someone to talk to ... take to the movies ... drink coffee with?*

"Hey, James," my friend Jared said the next day. "How'd you like the number of a singles line?"

UNMASKED

"What for?" I asked.

"You call and leave a profile and your number, and they match you up with some ladies," he explained.

I shrugged.

May as well try it.

I got the number of a lady who lived 30 miles away.

"How would you like to go out for coffee?" I asked when I called her. I named a restaurant halfway between our towns.

"I'd be delighted," Bunny responded.

"Here's the deal." I hastened to explain in case she didn't cotton to dating a motorcycle-riding-two-step-dancing ex-con. "I'll be wearing a black cowboy hat and Levi's. If you don't like what you see, just turn around and leave. I'll be none the wiser for it."

She came, liked what she saw and sat down.

"How would you like to go dancing?" I asked some four hours later.

"Sounds fun," Bunny replied.

I drove to a cowboy club, and we ordered cokes. My heart pounded at the opportunity to enjoy the club atmosphere and dancing after a 10-year sabbatical in the pen.

We circled the floor one time. Then I took Bunny's hand and led her to the door.

"Just not my cup of tea anymore," I explained to the unasked questions in her eyes. "I reckon God took all the desire from me."

I gave her hand a gentle squeeze. "I'm glad he did."

REBEL RIDER

"I'm glad, too," she replied. "I don't like it, either."

We married four months later.

Cycles for Christ

I learned of the Tribe of Judah Motorcycle Ministries and started to ride with them. The Tribe's focus is to bring the love of Jesus to outlaw biker bands. It felt good to have a bike under me again and feel the wind lifting my hair and stress from my shoulders.

I met a fellow rider named Kenny Martin. We met on a benefit ride for a buddy who'd taken a fall and carried no medical insurance.

One day, another rider-buddy, Bobby, called my home at 8 a.m. on a Sunday morning.

"Come to church with me this morning," he urged. "I know Bunny's working today."

"I'm supposed to ride with the Tribe this morning," I said.

"Okay. Let me know if you change your mind," Bobby said and hung up.

I swung my leg over my Harley. My fingers wrapped themselves around the handlebars.

Lord, what do you want me to do? I asked. *Where do you want me to go?*

I put the bike in gear and rode to the end of our subdivision. A left turn put me on the road to the Tribe. My bike leaned right. I turned that direction, stopped at a service station and called Bobby.

UNMASKED

"Okay," I said. "I guess God wants me to come with you this morning. Tell me how to get there."

He named a rendezvous location.

"You're going to love PK," he said when we met.

I approached the church in garb far different from my dude-dress-up-days, wearing an old ragged denim vest, head wrap, ponytail and beard.

The first thing I noticed was four other bikes parked by the door. My heart lifted. *Might not be so bad after all.*

Bobby ushered me to the door. The lady greeter grabbed me in a bear hug. "Welcome!" she exclaimed. Other people surrounded this hardcore-biker-ex-con, shook my hand and hugged me, each expressing genuine pleasure in meeting me.

"There's PK!" Bobby announced, waving at a man exiting the prayer room.

I did a double take. "That's Kenny Martin," I said.

"Huh?" Bobby said. "Around here, we call him PK, for Pastor Kenny."

PK rushed to close the space between us. "God told me you were coming today!" he exclaimed. "We have a biker group here at the church — Hard Core Christian Riders. I hope you'll come ride with us."

Boots on the Ground

Last Memorial Day I participated in a ceremony honoring our war dead. Eighteen war veterans and I circled a table known as the Lost Soldiers Memorial, on which a plate lay with a single grape on it. A glass sat by the plate. A bouquet of flowers, Bible and flag completed the table's setting.

"The glass is turned upside down," I explained to the large audience, "because the Lost Soldier can't drink from it. He can't drink from it, because he's not here." I paused.

"The single grape represents the food he died for so I can eat."

Silence permeated the scene.

"The flowers are here as a memorial of his sacrifice. The Lost Soldier died for my freedom — and yours." I choked back a tear.

"Let us stand and salute the flag."

Eighteen vets and 1,000 onlookers raised their voices to salute the flag in honor of the men and women who've laid down their lives so Americans can continue to live in freedom.

"… One nation, under God, indivisible, with liberty and justice for all."

Just like you, Jesus. Tears filled my eyes. *You died for my freedom. You drank the cup of wrath, so I go free. You tasted the bitterness of death to offer me life. Thank you, Jesus. I'll never forget your sacrifice.*

Never.

I swing my leg over my 2003 Harley-Davidson Dyna Low-Rider and wrap my fingers around the handles. *Perfect fit.* I grin.

Like you and me, Jesus.

UNMASKED

I inhale the heady mix of hot Texas air and Harley fumes as I tighten my bandana about my head. *You redeemed this rebel to cruise for you.*

I rev the engine a bit — and turn the wheel toward home.

CONCLUSION

A song was released in 1981 and went nine times platinum in the same year. It is the most requested song in karaoke everywhere. The reason, I believe, is because of how it speaks for people everywhere.

Just a small town girl, livin' in a lonely world
She took the midnight train goin' anywhere
Just a city boy, born and raised in south Detroit
He took the midnight train goin' anywhere

Chorus:
Don't stop believin'
Hold on to the feelin'
Streetlight people
Ohhhhhhh
Don't stop believin'

If you couldn't already guess, the band is Journey. I believe it's popular because we all hide somewhere in the night, because in the night the chance of revealing what is hurting is slim.

As we go through life, we are hurt and disappointed. Even though we do not want to stop believing, our hearts harden more and more. Then we put on masks. Masks to get us through when our insides are crying out to find emotion, to find relief, to find purpose.

UNMASKED

When I became a pastor, my heart broke for those who are hurting, who have felt as if they had to hide in the shadows, getting on any train heading anywhere. "Oh, you don't understand what I am going through." I hear this all the time, and really, I understand. You see, my story is in this book, too. I know that life can really look like there is no hope. I wanted life to end once, too.

We share these stories to give you hope in your heart — that you will know there is a God who is interested and concerned about *you personally.* The people in these stories have learned what it is like to become free, and they want you to know that you, too, can be set free.

At the Upper Room, our vision is to get to know you in the community, to radically become involved in your lives. Think about it: *How radical is giving you a book with our very personal stories in it?* We want you to know that your life can change. We believe God himself led the person to give you this book, if that's how you got it.

Why? you ask. Because he cares about you and your situation.

Everyone at the Upper Room wants you to come and see yourself as God sees you. When you come, you will be among the very people in this book. You may not recognize them because they are average men and women. Some have tattoos, some have long hair, some have no hair, some ride Harleys and wear leather vests and some drive Lexuses. The one thing that they all have in common is that they have experienced radical change in their life and have experienced hope, grace, love and acceptance.

CONCLUSION

Not to mention a great place to hang out and drink some amazing coffee! And they all found the answers to their sufferings in a personal relationship with Jesus Christ.

Come, ask questions, examine our reality factor and, if you choose, take that journey of unmasking with us at whatever pace you are comfortable with. We want you to know God is still completing the process of real life, life without masks in us. Now, we still make mistakes in our journey — everyone will. But by acknowledging the fact that we are not perfect, we also acknowledge our need for each others' forgiveness and support.

Jesus said, "I came that you may have and enjoy life, and have it in abundance [to the full, till it overflows]" (John 10:10b). In other words, it is Jesus' desire that your life journey be filled with peace, hope and joy, even while you are in the middle of a crisis or problems. The only way to experience that abundant life is to have a personal relationship with him.

Jesus wants you to have a life change just like those people you read about in this book.

The thing that holds us back from that personal relationship with Jesus is sin. Sin is anything we think, do or say that is against what God wants for us. The Bible teaches us that the wages of sin is death. All of us have had people sin against us — that is, do things to us that hurt us and drive us away from the abundant life God wants us to have. We then protect ourselves, becoming withdrawn and not trusting anyone. That has caused us to "die" emotionally and spiritually. When we died, hope, joy, our

UNMASKED

self-esteem and confidence also all died inside of us because of sin.

When Jesus died on the cross, he took our sin, our pains and our sorrows with him on that cross. He suffered a painful death so that we could be free and forgiven. All you have to do is receive what he did.

It would be like me having an envelope with $1,000 in it, and I tell you it is yours, and I put it on a table across the room. It doesn't become yours until you get up, walk over and take the envelope. Freedom and forgiveness is yours. All you have to do is take it.

If you are tired of wearing a mask, putting on a front, pretending nothing ever happened, freedom is yours through Jesus Christ. If you want this freedom, pray this simple prayer:

Jesus, I know that I am separated from you, that I have been wearing this mask for so long, but I want to change that. I am sorry for the choices that I have made; please forgive me. I need your help because I cannot fix my life. I believe your death paid for my sins and that you are now alive to change me from the inside out. Please do that for me now. I receive your love, your forgiveness, your cleansing. Make me brand new.

Thank you for hearing me and changing me. Come and live in me so that I know you are here with me. Now, please help me so I can know when you are talking to me so that I can cooperate with you to change me. Amen.

CONCLUSION

If you prayed that prayer, you have taken the first step toward your new walk in life. It is a walk of freedom. I personally invite you to come to Upper Room Fellowship Church where you will be loved and where you will learn how to continue in your walk of freedom and into the destiny that God has for you. You can listen to the messages on www.upperroomfc.org, and you can email us at info@upperroomfc.org.

We look forward to seeing you soon!

In Christ,
Kenny Martin
Senior Pastor
Upper Room Fellowship Church

SPECIAL THANKS

We commend each of those who through long hours and staying on top of things made this book a possibility. However, this book is dedicated to all of those people out there who, for various reasons, have felt that they have to hold up an image or strength or a certain status. Our primary purpose for this book is you. To encourage and provide hope for you. Whatever your circumstances may be, we want you to know there is hope.

We thank the storytellers for their honesty and for being transparent. We also thank each of the writers who not only captured the hearts of each of these testimonies, but also for relaying it in a way that assures each reader that there is hope.

I want to also thank Good Catch Publishing for all of your encouragement, guidance and direction for this book to be a reality.

Most importantly, I want to thank the One who has taken our need for masks away and replaced them with love, hope, peace and above all joy.

Kenny and Virginia Martin
Senior Pastors
Upper Room Fellowship Church

We would love for you to join us!

We meet Sunday mornings at 10:45 a.m. at
3636 Honea Egypt Road, Montgomery, TX 77316.

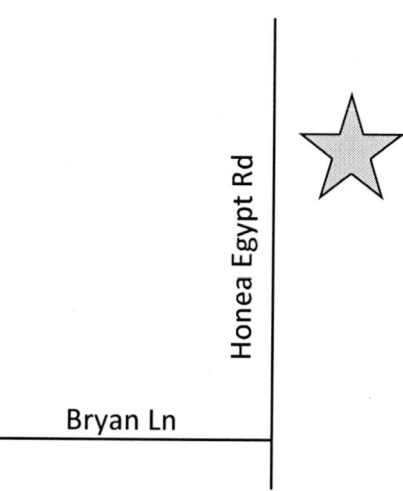

Please call us at 936.447.9813 for directions, or
contact us at www.upperroomfc.org.

For more information on reaching your city with stories from your church, please contact Good Catch Publishing at www.goodcatchpublishing.com

GOOD CATCH PUBLISHING

Did one of these stories touch you?
Did one of these real people move you to tears?
Tell us (and them) about it on our reader blog at
www.goodcatchpublishing.blogspot.com.